D1001401

We The Homeless
Portraits of America's Displaced People

We The P

Portraits of America's Displaced People

Homeless

Photographs by Stephenie Hollyman

Text by Victoria Irwin
with an Introduction by Robert M. Hayes

Designed by Michael Bierut

Philosophical Library, Inc., New York

To all of those who are working to give the homeless housing, jobs and hope.

*Project Manager: Jane Lahr
Enterprises*

Edited by Jane Bassin

**Library of Congress
Cataloging-in-Publication
Data**

Hollyman, Stephenie, 1952-
We the homeless.

1. Homeless persons—
United States.   2. Homeless
persons—United States—
Pictorial works. I. Irwin,
Victoria, 1954-
HV4505.H64 1988 362.5'0973
88-4158
ISBN 0-8022-2542-x

Published by Philosophical
Library, Inc.
200 West 57th Street, New
York, New York 10019

Printed and bound in the
United State of America.

Acknowledgments

So many people helped in the making of this book that it is impossible to thank all of them individually in this small space, especially the many friends, editors, colleagues and family who gave me opportunities and encouragement.

I want to thank my publishers Rose Runes and Ginger Najar for a commitment to informing the public about the plight of the homeless that went far beyond commercial publishing goals. I owe a very special thank you to Michael Bierut of Vignelli Associates, designer of *We The Homeless*, for his sensitivity, extraordinary talent, and the time which he so generously donated. Thanks also to Jane Lahr and Jane Bassin for overseeing this project.

Many thanks to Carlo Mastricolo, former Assignments Editor for *The New York Times*, now with *The Boston Globe*. His phone call one Friday night in 1985 to photograph homeless mothers set me off on this extended self-assignment that lasted for three years. Thank you to Carolyn Lee of *The New York Times*.

There were a number of people for whose contribution of materials and equipment I am very grateful: Bill Geizendanner at Ilford Photo for the donation of film; Chrysler's loan of a van for the Appalachia portion of the book; David Schlink at E. Leitz Inc. for loaning me the superb Leica M-6 system; Anne-Lise Spector at Random Audio Books whose supply of books-on-tape kept me entertained as I drove 15,000 miles around the United States.

In October of 1987, these photographs were exhibited for the first time in a show at the Senate Rotunda in Washington. I want to thank Senator Daniel Patrick Moynihan for sponsoring the show. Thanks also to Dorian Friedman, and Sean Callahan of Sen. Moynihan's office; to Laurie Fishler, Tom Franz, and Mark Jackson for their help; to Joan Carroll Design for use of her Instand panels; and to Frederick Allen of J.P. Morgan & Co. Incorporated for making it a reality.

Thanks to Rufus Jones, resident of the now-defunct Los Angeles Urban Encampment, for permitting me to use his poem "I Can See the Tears."

My deepest debt of gratitude is owed to those on the front lines of the homeless crisis, the homeless who so generously opened their lives to me and to the dedicated advocates who took time from their duties to help me get my photographs, feed me an occasional meal, fuel my sometimes flagging spirits and who, by their example, kept me trucking down the road. To all of you, thank you, especially: Lynette Stuart, Big Stone Gap, VA; Ralph Di Palma, Albuquerque, NM; Millard Fuller, Americus, GA; "Mohawk," Lexington, KY; Tom Holy, Tulsa, OK; Gretchen Buchenholz, New York, NY; The Community of Coahoma, MS; Sister Connie Driscoll, Chicago, IL; Mary Ann Gleason, Denver, CO; Brother Paul Johnson, Miami, FL; Louisa Stark, Phoenix, AZ; Sally McCabe, Albuquerque, NM; Robert M. Hayes, New York, NY; John Lozier and "Bear," Nashville, TN; Gary Blasie, Los Angeles, CA; Cindy Bogner, New York, NY; Audrey Williams and family, New York, NY; Mitch Snyder and Mary Ellen Holmes, Washington, DC.

Stephenie Hollyman

Introduction
by Robert M. Hayes,
Coalition for the Homeless

erhaps it's all an experiment," said the old woman, bundled in tattered rags at New York City's Pennsylvania Station one night in late 1979. "Perhaps they're trying to find out just how long we can live out here, how long we can survive, without food, without shelter.

"It's got to be an experiment," she said. "What else could explain it?"

That is the question which must haunt any reader of Stephenie Hollyman's epic "We The Homeless," as this grand national experiment of mass, contemporary homelessness nears the end of its first decade.

I do not know what became of that old woman in Penn Station whose words touched the few who heard her. But, I dread to say, I have a pretty good idea.

Homelessness creeps over its victims like T.S. Eliot's yellow smoke. First, you recognize that something is wrong in your life and suddenly you—and maybe your family too—are on the streets. You're in shock. It's a catastrophe to you, but nobody else seems to notice. And death—early, gratuitous and unnecessary—creeps in too. It's as common to those people who live in the streets as that studied glance away most Americans instinctively develop when a homeless person appears in their path.

We say to ourselves, "What if he assaults me?" But we fear something perhaps more threatening: "What if he looks me in the eye and asks me for help?"

A slow, grinding death is the inevitable consequence of our grand experiment of homelessness, and the invisibility of life follows the homeless to their deaths.

There is no national cemetery with neat rows of white tombstones for the army of the homeless. In death comes the final, and typical indignity: a crude burial with dozens of other corpses in an open trench in some windswept Potter's Field.

y own journey follows the map laid out by Stephenie Hollyman. In the late 1970s, finding what I thought was a local aberration unique to New York, I stumbled onto the scandal of government complicity in the barbarism of New York's Bowery.

And over time the battle that began there for decent shelter, affordable housing, and sufficient food extended like a pervasive refrain from Guthrie's "This Land is Your Land," to the deserts of the southwest, to the Pacific coast, to the mountains of Appalachia, to the *barrios* of Miami.

As the same story was repeated, time after time, my memory flashed back to a former short-order cook I knew on the Bowery. The simple photographs of "We the Homeless" stir for me the same memory. The memory is of a man, an imperfect man, a homeless man, and a friend. His name was Robert Callahan.

Callahan was a man who, for 50 years, led a very unremarkable American life. For his last five years he led an existence of extraordinary deprivation on the streets of New York City.

Callahan—he would never respond to Bob, or Robert or, God forbid, Mister—was born in Brooklyn in 1925, and was reared in an Irish Catholic family. He graduated from high school, joined the U.S. Army, and served in Italy just after the war. Then he came home.

He became a short-order cook, frying eggs, hamburgers and hash browns in a number of restaurants. He did his work faithfully for several decades. Later on I tasted Callahan's cooking. It wasn't great, but it wasn't horrible. Callahan taught me how to flip an egg. It was unclear who was to blame, but years later there was still some egg stuck behind my stove.

In the early 1970s Callahan tired of cooking. He traveled through the South, working from time to time as a gardener. At heart, though, he was a New Yorker. So he came home again. He found an apartment but could not find a job. By 1975 it seems there was no need in Brooklyn for a 50 year old short-order cook.

Callahan couldn't make his rent. He took to drink, he got evicted, and suddenly—at age 50—he was homeless.

From here on, by any civilized standard, Callahan's story becomes extraordinary. But to folks who are homeless, this too is a familiar tale.

Callahan went to a welfare office in Brooklyn. He told the worker that he was broke, evicted and needed help. "You're a bum," the worker said. Callahan blanched. He was told to go to a men's shelter.

I don't know what went through Callahan's mind that afternoon as he walked across the Brooklyn Bridge to get to New York City's Bowery shelter.

But I know what Callahan saw at the shelter. He saw 1,000 men lined up for the gruel called dinner. He was offered floor space in the shelter's "big room" along with 200 other men. That night, Callahan ran from the men's shelter. He walked all night, and the next night, and the next night. But it was winter, and it was cold. Within a week he was sleeping on a newspaper on the floor at the men's shelter. He was drinking more.

Callahan adapted, sort of. We met. I was a lawyer newly admitted to the bar, who carried with me the baggage of Wall Street's most prestigious law firm. Callahan became my guide to the Bowery.

There were tricks to learn. If one sneaked into a mission at the right time you could get a bowl of soup, and avoid the sermon. He knew about the bathrooms in the courthouses. He knew which grates blew dry heat; he knew park benches that were, well, pretty safe.

He had the pride and the sense, back there in 1979, to avoid the men's shelter except in the dead of winter. He liked to be called the "Mayor of the Bowery" though to most of his friends he was Callahan.

In the fall of 1979 it was clear to me that only a lawsuit would move the City to help the homeless. Persuasion had not worked. Callahan was the obvious candidate to stand up in the suit against Governor Carey and Mayor Koch. So the suit was brought: Robert Callahan, on his own behalf and on behalf of all others similarly situated, against Hugh L. Carey, as governor of the State of New York, and Edward I. Koch, as mayor of the City of New York.

He worked hard on the suit, scouting for evidence, telling me what I should be doing, telling me how I should be doing it. Vignettes of that time with Callahan come back to me.

I remember a strategy session we held with another lawyer helping on the case. My colleague took out an expensive, imported Dunhill cigarette to light, saw Callahan eye it, and offered him one. He looked at the Dunhill, smelled it, bit off the filter, and lit it up. Callahan enjoyed those moments when Wall Street met the Bowery. The meetings were always on his terms.

I remember his anger when the *New York Post* ran his picture on the court house steps under a headline: "Bowery Bum in Court." Callahan was very angry. If there were any bums in this lawsuit, he told me, the bums were the defendants. He meant the Governor and the Mayor. Mr. Callahan was right: he was no bum.

I remember the week before Christmas. Callahan had moved in with me for a time. Then the Long Island Railroad went on strike and a high school friend, a quiet and shy actuary, moved in too. It was tight quarters, the three of us in one room. I avoided the place, coming home to snores late at night.

It was only weeks later that I found out Callahan had been reigning supreme. Each night when the actuary arrived home, Callahan handed him a shopping list. Dutifully, the actuary went to the store, bought the groceries and watched Callahan cook up a storm. Those were good times for Callahan.

It was Christmas Eve that year that Callahan had his first big victory. A State Supreme Court judge, ruling in the case of *Callahan v. Carey*, held that the homeless in New York have a right to shelter. I found Callahan in a

13

Bowery flophouse and told him the news. "Callahan over Carey," he said, "isn't it great? The right Irishman won."

Things did not go well for Callahan after that. That winter's court victory was an empty one for Callahan. The court only ordered the city to provide shelter; the court did not say what the shelter had to be like. So the wretched conditions continued, and Callahan spent most of his nights on the street.

He was getting thinner, as winter became summer, and his spirits were sagging. The last time I saw Callahan was in September at Penn Station. Winter was returning to the Northeast. I put him on a train east; he felt sure he could rest up with some friends on Long Island.

I don't know if he ever got there. I heard nothing for several weeks. Then on a Wednesday evening I got a call: Callahan had been found, face down, on Mott Street. He simply collapsed, and died. He died alone.

No autopsy was done. The medical examiner filed a death certificate. The cause of death? "Natural causes," the City certificate says.

Maybe it's wrong, now, in the late 1980s, to talk of Callahan when we think of the homeless. In many cities now, young children are the fastest growing group of homeless people.

And just as Callahan died, I have seen the death of children from homelessness. More often I have seen childhood, supposedly that time of innocence and joy, robbed too soon and too painfully from little girls and boys.

But Callahan does represent the homeless: his life was beautiful and it was ugly; his life was courageous and it was cowardly; his life, like the lives captured by Stephenie Hollyman's camera, was human. All too human.

That is the message of this book: the humanity of "We the Homeless." Robert Callahan, the people in this book, and the people living on streets across America, are all human beings, filled with frailties, imperfections, and faults.

Like Callahan, they face an untimely death, and the final blow of some medical examiner ruling that death is due to natural causes.

Neither Callahan nor other homeless Americans are dying of natural causes. They die because they are homeless, and that is as unnatural and uncivilized a state as there can be. They are homeless because there is nowhere decent inside for America's Callahans. And there is no place inside because we, as a rich people in a rich nation, do not care enough to insist that decent shelter be provided.

The portraits of America's homeless in this volume should become Exhibit A in decency's call that housing for America's homeless is the moral imperative for a civilized land.

But in the beauty of the humanity that is captured here, there is a risk. It's the same risk as fondly remembering Robert Callahan as a man who led a life of romance when in fact his was a life of great misery.

As you see the strength in the wizened faces of old homeless men photographed here, do not be mistaken. Homelessness is not a romance that builds character.

And as you see the maternal love etched in the eyes of a homeless mother nursing her homeless child, do not be mistaken. Homelessness is not a romance that strengthens family bonds.

And as you see the magic in the smile of a homeless little girl, do not be mistaken. Homelessness does not nurture the growing child.

Stephenie Hollyman's work is a portrait of human resilience. It captures a human tragedy. It is not a nice book.

For homelessness, when you honestly see it, is not picturesque.

It is evidence of an experiment gone mad.

We The Homeless
by Victoria Irwin

T he setting changes, but it's the same story. In Chicago, a Hispanic boy plays in the twilight on the sidewalk while his mother begs for money. In Denver, an employed father and mother live in a shelter because they can't afford an apartment. Saturday afternoon strollers in New York step over an alcoholic man who passed out on the sidewalk in front of a building being rehabilitated as condominiums.

These people are members of a new and growing minority in America that, perhaps more than any other disadvantaged group, is making all of us question who we are as a people. We call them the homeless. No one really knows how many there are, but depending on which estimate you read, there are between 350,000 and 2,000,000 Americans without permanent roofs over their heads. The U.S. Conference of Mayors reported a 21% increase in the number of homeless in 26 surveyed cities in 1987.

Homelessness. It's a state of being we usually associate with bag ladies and derelicts, drunks and addicts. However, a third of the homeless in the United States today are children and their parents. Very few parents in homeless families suffer from mental health problems, but a small portion do have drug- and alcohol-related problems. Roughly another third of the homeless are the chronically mentally ill, those who sit in tattered clothes, speaking to unseen companions, often in poor health, often the victims of crime. It is also true that some 30-40% of the homeless are substance abusers, panhandling on street corners for the wherewithal to sustain alcohol or drug habits.

These are the "visible" homeless, the ones that create in us a complex rush of feeling, including anger, compassion, fear, confusion, guilt, and, finally, indifference. The harsh fact is that the fastest growing category of homeless Americans are the "invisible" homeless, the ones we don't notice because they don't look very different from us. They are single mothers with pre-school children who lost their run-down apartments because of fire; families with husbands and fathers who lost their jobs as more and more factories closed down; abused women escaping to shelters with their children; and young veterans returning from the military with no marketable skills. There are the elderly on fixed incomes who have been evicted as neighborhoods gentrify, and families on welfare who don't have enough money to pay for both rent and food.

Education, that magic substance that was supposed to be a panacea against poverty, has lost its protective powers. Half the homeless have high school diplomas and 25-30% have attended college. Not all of the homeless are unemployed. But even if they do work, they can't find safe, decent housing that they can afford. In cities across the United States, shelter providers and meal program directors say they are seeing more and more families, more and more children. Most of the homeless are single, but in a disturbing trend, the faces of the homeless are getting younger and younger.

Homelessness is not simply an urban phenomenon. Here, in one of the richest countries on earth, there is hardly a community that does not have a Vietnam veteran, a bag lady, or a family without a home. Why is this happening? The causes are as diverse as the homeless themselves. Most important are the inadequate stock of decent, affordable housing, and incomes so low that they can't meet even the most basic of needs.

But there are other factors involved. The mentally ill homeless have been deinstitutionalized into a society that does not provide follow-up services. Vietnam veterans, who are found in alarming numbers on the street, say they have not been helped by the Veterans Administration. Some homeless families come from generations of poverty, and the parents have few work skills. For some homeless, it is simply that the economy in certain areas has gone bust.

Although conditions are not as desperate as those faced by their counterparts in the Third World, the homeless in America face similar dilemmas—lack of affordable and safe housing, lack of jobs, inadequate work skills in an economy that seems prepared to pass them by, occasional employment at a minimum wage that can't come close to making ends meet. They must cope with family breakups, high crime rate, discrimination, racism, poor education, drug and alcohol abuse. These citizens, who have captured Congressional attention but have little actual political clout, often lack such basics as adequate food, physical and mental health care, and transportation.

And further, American society—from politicians to average citizens—has not yet come to terms with how to deal with the homeless. Emergency shelter is needed, but some fear it is becoming the accepted low-income housing of the future. Lip service is given to building permanent low-cost homes, but Congress could not pass a housing bill from 1981 to 1987.

A home of one's own is part of the American dream, but that dream has become nearly impossible for too many Americans. Low-income housing has virtually disappeared, due to shrinking federal aid, low vacancy rates in some cities, and massive arson and abandonment in other urban areas. Ironically, some cities have plenty of housing, but a sour economy puts it out of reach for the jobless.

There is talk of a new national housing policy. But advocates for the homeless speak in even stronger terms—of a right to housing, as opposed to "right housing when available."

Whether or not there is agreement on the causes or solutions for homelessness, no one disputes that the number of homeless Americans continues to grow. Every day, in small towns and bustling cities, the homeless welcome new members to their ranks. Poverty, they discover, is egalitarian—the homeless are black, white, Hispanic, Asian, native American.

Many of the homeless are uncomfortably visible on the streets of our major cities. But many more pass through society almost unnoticed, making the best use they can of the scant resources available to them, including relatives and friends. Families living with other families have earned the sobriquet "couch people" from sociologists and journalists. They are a far cry from the latest baby-boom phenomenon called "couch potatoes," those who stay in their own homes,

insulated from the world, and watch television. Homeless couch people are those who literally sleep on the couch, often feeling like intruders, often sharing meager resources in substandard housing. A rural Mississippi family with four children and assorted relatives shares two beds and a couch in a house that is well below safety standards. In New York City there are an estimated 100,000 couch people. Many will end up in shelters as pressure increases.

Men, women, and some children sleep in parks, both urban and rural, to avoid the frisking—strip searches in some cases—and angry questions they often face when coming into large public shelters. Inside, cots or plain mattresses on the floor do not mean a peaceful night's rest, even in the best-managed shelters. Fights break out among the tumultuous and emotionally ragged residents. The very guards hired to ensure safety have sometimes attacked residents. Clothing and personal belongings can be stolen in an instant.

In big cities, the homeless often live in crime-infested welfare hotels, placed there by officials who have not been able to come to grips with the lack of affordable housing. A child's first steps in a New York welfare hotel may be down a hallway past crack dealers. At rates as high as $3000 a month, families stay more than a year in such hotels. Cutbacks in Federal funding have hurt the construction of low-income housing and money is being funneled into shelters and transitional housing. Some permanent homes are being built or rehabilitated, but the need far outpaces the supply.

In the land that invented it, the automobile has taken on new significance. The new poor live in cars, camp by rivers and stay with friends until their welcome wears out as they travel the roads looking for work. A small girl in Texas, who knows the routine, hands her father a lug wrench at the right moment as he changes a tire during the family's nation-wide trek in search of work and shelter. Abandoned vehicles—cars, buses, truck containers—are being pressed into service as temporary homes. Moved constantly from neighborhood to neighborhood if not from city to city, children attend school only sporadically. There are toddlers whose parents have never baked them a birthday cake because they have never lived long enough in a place with an oven.

The tracks of the homeless are often hard to spot, at first. You can find them, if you look. They are at McDonald's, where a mother watches her children in the playground and waits for the "old" hamburgers to be put out in the garbage. You see them at free movies at public libraries, where so-called bag ladies safely and warmly catch up on much-needed sleep. A family walking along the shoulder of a narrow upstate New York road is homeless; they walk the two mile journey to a convenience store because they don't have a car. They are hard to spot because they look like us.

We are the homeless. The homeless are us.

Two Oklahomans work in the fierce midday sun outside Tulsa, their car temporarily immobile as they replace one frayed tire with a fifteen-dollar retread.

"It's kind of discouraging," says Rob, while her husband Mike wrestles with the tire. They've just spent the night in sleeping bags on the ground by Keystone Lake outside Tulsa.

Most of their valuables—clothes, ice chest, tools, dishes, sentimental items—are packed into their car while the couple travels between cities trying to find construction work for Mike. They have been camping out for a week and a half, returning from Houston. There haven't been any jobs anywhere.

"I just don't think it's right for our Congressman, our Senators, and our President to be sitting up there in their mighty offices, and they have food on the table every day, clothes on their back, and don't have a worry in the world," says Rob. "And then they have the nerve to say this country is not in bad shape. They are liars. They need to be out here on the street with everybody else."

Rob and Mike see themselves as victims of an economy that has taken a down turn and a government that has not been fair to the working people. They are among the thousands of homeless who do not fit into the easy categorization of the homeless as the "underclass"— a term that has gained acceptance in the media, but not among the poor themselves, either the new or "old" poor. "Me, I don't have any kind of trade," says Rob. "It makes it kind of hard for me. We had an apartment. Work slowed down, and we couldn't afford to pay rent." Michael is in construction, and "when construction is down, money stops coming in. I think this government could produce more jobs for working people," he offers.

Mike and Rob face a predicament that is increasingly familiar among America's blue-collar workers. As the U.S. economy shifts from heavy industry to an emphasis on the service sector and high technology, workers find themselves changing jobs—and occupations—with regularity. Even with unemployment down, there are thousands who are underemployed or out of the job market altogether. Many job postings call for specialized skills in computers, electronics, health care, or financial management, or offer minimum wage, part-time work. Many heavy-industry workers—employees from steel or farm equipment plants—now find themselves in jobs that pay less than before.

Retraining programs have only spotty success. There are a surprising number of homeless who have gone through computer schools designed to get them entry-level jobs; advocates charge that some of these institutions bilk both the students and the government, which usually pays for the training. And even the federal employment service admits its record at helping so-called dislocated workers is bad—only one in twenty gets work through the government agency.

Many of the poorest of the homeless come from several generations of poverty. They worked at low-skill manufacturing jobs mostly in urban areas. The slow and continuing erosion of this source of employment and the decaying housing stock are two long-term factors contributing to the increased vulnerability of this group of Americans.

But the cutoff of benefits to these working poor has seriously exacerbated an already bad situation. Most advocates say they can trace the great increase in homelessness to both the recession of the early eighties and to the cuts

in federal aid programs that took place in the administration of Ronald Reagan.

A case in point is that of Laverne who lives in Washington, D.C. She worked for many years before she recently got behind on her utility bill. She sought help from a social service system that kept sending her to different agencies, each telling her she wasn't eligible for help.

"I was trying to do the right thing," says Laverne in exasperation. The utilities were cut off, and she lost her home. Unable to find a new apartment for herself and her four children, she went to a shelter. One of the stipulations of the shelter was that she actively look for an apartment, which meant she had to take time off from work. Laverne lost her job.

Today, Laverne and her family are in a transitional housing program, but not until after "a lot of bad changes" happened to the kids, she says. And Laverne says it has taken a lot for her to regain self-esteem.

Another segment of newly homeless are those whose service-oriented businesses went under when harder times made people decide to do without conveniences.

Dee moved in with her mother when she lost her dog-grooming business. Her Oklahoma clients dropped away as they tightened their belts in the oil slump.

Her son sleeps on the couch in the living room. She has a mattress on the floor in another room; it's so small she has to lean the mattress up against the wall to get out in the morning. Her boyfriend, who helps her with money, is living in his pickup truck. They had hoped to get a house together.

These are America's new poor. They are also homeless and for all of them the strains are the same.

"They still want to work, they also want to have a home," says Bud Roth, a volunteer job counselor in a Denver shelter. "In this land of plenty, to have all these folks out there just trying to get by! . . . They are not the hoboes and bums and the derelicts. They've had homes, they've had jobs. Factories have closed. Oil businesses have shut down. It's a sad time."

19

The stories of the homeless sound eerily familiar, tragedies that happen in many families in cities, in suburbs, in small towns. Most Americans have resources to fall back on when they hit hard times. The homeless, for a variety of reasons, have fallen through the cracks. The safety net that was woven is now in shreds. Both the government and society have failed the homeless.

"The common characteristic is disaffiliation," says Andy Raubeson, executive director of the Single Room Occupany Housing Corporation in Los Angeles. Whether it is substance abuse, mental illness, family breakups, or economic circumstances, these are people who do not have normal ties to family or community. Or their family or community is too broken themselves to offer much help.

"If there is any underlying fact among all of these people, it's a lack of support or love in the home," says Bud Roth. "A lack of a sense of a value in life."

This loss of worth and self-esteem is heard frequently in conversations with the homeless.

"My family doesn't want anything to do with me," says one man in Denver, who sleeps on the streets when he can't get in a shelter. "I can't say I blame them much. But it's the truth."

In a semi-dark room at a Milwaukee Salvation Army shelter, Gloria sits on the edge of the bed where her pre-school age son is sleeping. Her parents—and a college-age daughter—are in Atlanta, but she is not certain she wants to return to them. Today she is unemployed and trying to escape an abusive relationship. They are disappointed, Gloria explains, because she never finished college.

"It's a weird situation," says Gloria, who seems infinitely tired. "My father had great hopes for me. Most of my people are college graduates."

When she returned home in the past, her relatives asked her why she hadn't done well after all they had done for her.

"When I ask for help, I have to go through all that," says Gloria. "They won't let me forget it. I'm not the worst person. I didn't get an

20

education, but why regard me as a nobody? Families are getting to be strangers to each other."

Some families continue to keep in touch. In urban areas, many homeless live doubled up with relatives for long periods of time before they leave, sometimes because the landlord threatens eviction of the whole family unless the "guests" move out. In shelters, there are many mothers whose families are split up. In Chicago, Mary stays in a noisy but genial family shelter with her two youngest sons, one a three-month-old baby. Her oldest son lives with her mother, and they talk on the phone or visit daily.

But other homeless come from shattered families. In shelters and on the streets, they say they haven't talked to their family in years. Sometimes they say they are ashamed of themselves. Sometimes they simply don't want to see their family.

Despite the shattered family ties, there is a camaraderie among many homeless that is strong and touching. Shelters can be tolerable as a community in which, however briefly, they can laugh at and share their plight. In the Los Angeles urban encampment that operated for several months in the summer and fall of 1987, twelve-year-old Segura Williams started a group for children living in the camp, poignantly speaking out for their rights.

In Denver, a homeless man describes how his feelings toward the poor have changed. He talks about the homeless as "them," even while admitting he is homeless. This third-person explanation of his plight is common.

"After being self-supporting, then finding yourself being one of those street people you see everyday and kind of avoid. . .you get a real tender outlook on those kind of people, because you are one, you are walking in their shoes."

Are the increasing numbers of homeless becoming an accepted institution in the United States? The man in Denver feels "tender" toward the homeless, in part because he is homeless. But while most Americans gasp at the increased visibility of the homeless, the responses do not always register outrage with the status quo. New shelters open and old ones are enlarged. The media daily chronicle their plight. In 1987, Congress passed a homeless assistance act appropriating $355-million in 1987 for emergency shelter, food, and other programs and services for the homeless. Funding is slated to go to $616-million in 1988.

But broader questions are not being asked. And the homeless continue to be thought of as "them" instead of us.

"I think this is the most radical form of poverty we've ever known," says Mary Ann Gleason, an advocate in Denver. She agrees that deep, philosophical questions need to be raised. Are we letting the institutional approach of shelters, modern-day almshouses, substitute for acceptable low-income housing? Will the U.S. accept a two-tiered society, or will this country work toward eradicating such divisions?

She even sees it among groups helping the homeless—in a decision by one group to build a $5-million shelter instead of permanent housing and vocational rehabilitation for the chronically mentally ill, for example. Using shelters merely to get the homeless off the streets is very short-sighted, says Gleason.

"My fear is that temporary shelter is seen as a solution, and is financed as the solution, and that sets up social policy. . . . We are not being reflective," says Gleason. "As long as these things are tolerable, something has gone seriously awry. This is moral-crisis time."

Coalitions spring up in most cities. Conferences are held among academics on the issues of health care, mental illness, the housing crisis. Politicians spend the night outdoors to dramatize the need for legislation. Nonprofit fundraisers tell small shelters how to do a direct-mail campaign in order to get funding. It is all very removed from the child playing in the glass-strewn dirt lot surrounded by a 12-foot Cyclone fence in the Los Angeles urban encampment, a tent city nicknamed the Dustbowl Hilton by its residents.

One often-stated axiom is that the poor and the homeless have always been with us. But this population is different. With the millions who were hungry, jobless, or homeless during the Great Depression, economic hardship crossed most social lines. The whole nation suffered, and the government helped to pull the nation up.

"During the Great Depression, the homeless had no way of earning a living," says Rodger Farr, a psychiatrist with the Los Angeles County Department of Mental Health. "Now unemployment is. . .[down], and the economy is doing well. But we have as many homeless now as we did in 1980 [when the last recession began]. What is happening to the economic cycles is not. . .[reducing the number of] the homeless."

Many homeless families find that the welfare system that is supposed to keep them afloat does not do much toward finding housing. They have battles on several fronts simultaneously: the search for a proper home, the daily routine of a disrupted family life, the search for work, the bureaucracy of the welfare system, frustration, and anger. And, the bottom line, their benefits do not stretch far enough.

In New York City, one mother reported giving her food stamps to her landlord to pay the balance of her rent, or else she would face eviction.

Advocates for the homeless also note an increase in the temporarily homeless, people whose welfare grants are gone before the end of the month. The lines at St. Benedict's meal program in Milwaukee swell at the end of the month, and become small after the checks have arrived. Many shelters report the same phenomena.

Those managing to get work at a minimum wage face a similar dilemma.

In Houston, outside the Star of Hope Mission, Bob changes a tire, the skyline of the city behind him, glass towers gleaming in the late afternoon light. As his small daughter assists him with the tire, Bob tells of the circuitous path he has taken looking for work. His plant in Illinois closed, and the whole family hit the road looking for work. They have been to Georgia, Arkansas, Louisianna, Tennessee, Mississippi, and Oklahoma.

"Ain't nobody can help you in Houston either," says Bob, as he sits on his haunches. "I work out of the labor hall here. $3.35 an hour. Any dirty job they want. Dig a ditch, pipeline, pick up garbage. It's more responsibility with a family. I have to make sure the kids are fed and have a place to spend the night."

In Denver, a father plays with his daughter on his lap. He smiles at her, but then turns a discouraged face to a visitor.

"There is no more ladder to move up on," he says. "We move out of here and go pay rent on a place, and we won't have enough money to afford anything else except gas and utilities. We have to get clothes for our daughter from Goodwill. We've already figured this up on what we're going to be making. You can scratch out moving up.

"The best we're going to be able to do is just get a roof over our heads," he says. "that's okay, but I want more, you see?"

Still, he says he is pretty sure he and his family will make it. He notes that it is easy, in shelters, to get used to expecting nothing. Being homeless is a rigorous life that no one enjoys.

"The impact of being homeless leaves a tremendous need for services," says Harry Kaplan, director of Homeless Services Network in Westchester County, New York. "The primary concern is where they are going to eat and sleep today. They have greatly reduced control over their lives."

They can't plan meals. Looking for a job or educational training becomes an arduous process when there is no access to child care, transportation, or even a quiet spot to spruce up and get prepared for a job interview.

And the loss of self-esteem can be devastating.

"I try not to let it get to me too much, because I find if I do, I can really get depressed," says Antoinette in Milwaukee, who says she looks at math textbooks at night when her three children are asleep, just to keep up with schooling. She dropped out of a nursing program when she fled an abusive relationship. "I want to keep a straight head."

"It's kind of hard taking help from people," says a homeless man. "It's a matter of pride, I guess. You really have to forget, get rid of all your dreams. You have dreams of going to college, getting an education, specializing in something. And then you lose everything and have to go on welfare. And you can put your dreams off a few more years."

Nearly one-fourth of all children in the United States under six years of age live in poverty, according to the U.S. Census Bureau. A growing number of these are also homeless, and so are their older brothers and sisters. Some advocates have come across children who have been homeless all their lives. What is life like for a homeless child?

On Chicago's South Side, Sister Connie Driscoll gives shelter to women and children in a clean if spartan dormitory setting. Each family has a small section to themselves, complete with bunk beds and lockers with the children's drawings taped on. Children can attend a parochial school across the street. Mothers take GED classes, learn kitchen skills, and—in a new program—are taught basics of living, such as landlord-tenant relations. Sister Connie says that many of the families here were evicted for nonpayment of rent, improper care of their apartments, or other disputes with a landlord.

In Poughkeepsie, New York, nine-year-old Raymond, who lives in a motel with his parents and two sisters, wants to be a policeman. Twelve-year-old Nathan, in a Seattle shelter with his father, wants to be a biologist. To Nathan, living in this family shelter in the shadow of the city's Space Needle is kind of an adventure. But as the spunky towhead talks about school, it is obvious he is painfully aware of his status, though he is a good student. And his care and concern for one-year-old Tiffany, the daughter of a teenage couple in the shelter, evinces a grown-up side many youngsters his age do not have.

Like children everywhere, homeless children can be cheerful and full of boisterious play. But there are subtle signs of bewilderment too. At a New York City community center with a special program for children who live in welfare hotels, the drawings by grade-schoolers can be stark.

One, for instance, is of a mother, brothers, and sisters, and in the background an apartment building has flames coming out of the window. In another drawing, a child has drawn a picture of a cat, scrawling underneath that the pet is now dead.

Ellen L. Bassuk, a Harvard Univerity Medical School psychiatrist, has studied homeless children. She says that preschool homeless often lag in major developmental milestones, such as walking, talking, and playing with building blocks. Among older homeless children, she encountered a significant degree of depression and anxiety.

"Almost every kid I talked to had thought about suicide," she says. There are often very few services available to these children. For example, only twenty percent of the preschoolers in her study had access to Head Start programs, universally viewed as a successful program for the poor.

In shelters, children are often hyperactive, sometimes the result of a high-sugar diet from the fast-food their mothers buy because there is no kitchen to prepare better food. Because they are often clustered with other young children, health problems can multiply more rapidly.

And homeless families are not always obviously homeless, because they try hard to stay invisible. In California, several advocates for the homeless note that in the past homeless families avoided seeking social services because of the fear that their children would be put in foster care. Laws have been strengthened to protect them. But the fear lingers.

Many families are not intact. In urban areas, where the homeless are often part of families that have been on welfare for generations, husbands are scarce. Mothers sometimes have

24

children from more than one father. Denise eats a healthy if bland dinner with her two babies, Sahkeda, three, and Arlina, two, in a noisy soup kitchen at St. Benedict's in Milwaukee. She bristles when a visitor comments on her lovely family.

"No, it's not. The family is not all here," says Denise, a high school dropout who explains that her oldest son and daughter are living with her parents. "I want them to be with me."

Dr. Bassuk says her studies show that family problems are complicated when women have little self-esteem or have been victims of abuse. Two-thirds of the homeless mothers in her survey came from disrupted homes. Most mothers do not have mental-health problems. But many have had housing difficulties for the past five years. Many had been in shelters before, or had doubled up or tripled up with friends and relatives.

Without financial assistance, housing, and a wide range of support services, these families move from one unstable situation to another, says Bassuk. From a policy point of view, shelters or interim housing is just another stop on a cycle.

Homeless parents find that in their day-to-day life they become "public parents." In shelters they are told when to get up, and if there is no daytime program they have to leave, sometimes as early as 6:30 A.M. Inadequate income leaves them dependent on providers.

Parents often have little say over where their children attend school. Homeless children from Westchester County in New York are sometimes cabbed an hour and a half to school. And motel and hotel owners put greater strictures on their homeless guests.

One motel owner in Westchester County slapped Joann's son Raymond as he was playing in the parking lot, because he thought the boy had scratched his automobile with a bicycle. Joann was angry, but she says she was helpless to complain. The only thing she could do was ask to leave the motel.

Joann sits in a new motel room with her long-time companion, Richard. Three of their children are sleeping in the two large beds—the youngest sleeps with her parents. The couple says their life is on hold. And they talk of what it is like to have most of their life public. Teachers ask their children questions about how they are treated at home, probing for potential abuse.

"They ask, does your mommy do this?" says Joann, a soft-spoken high school dropout who quit her job at a factory to take care of her youngest child. "They take it too far."

"Then they put a lot of pressure on us," says Richard, an unemployed dropout who failed to pass a general educational development test (GED). He wants to try it again before he enrolls in a job-training course.

Their oldest daughter is in foster care, because Joann was under "a lot of stress," says Richard. They visit her regularly. There is much warmth between the parents and the three youngest children. The couple, who live in a motel in Poughskeepsie, say they work hard to survive when things get tough.

"We just sit down and talk to one another," says Richard as four-year-old Shontay leans against his shoulder. "We do a lot of things with the family, try to get them to understand, let them know what is happening. We are both in this situation, not one."

Children are not the only homeless with heightened vulnerability and loneliness. Some of those most at risk, most cut off from possible help, are the chronically mentally ill who make up an estimated 35 to 50% of the homeless.

"The streets have become the mental asylums of the eighties," says Dr. Farr of the Los Angeles County Department of Mental Health.

In Griffith Park in Los Angeles, Judy lives in a camp in the wooded hills behind Hollywood. An almost elfin woman dressed in layers of clothes with a dog leash around her neck and a scarf over her head, she is initially hostile toward visitors, shaking the big stick she always carries.

But her eyes sparkle and she smiles as she shows her guests around her camp, arranged according to a "show script." Here, she says, is the "family circle," where "a mother and a six-

or eight-year-old" can sit around with guitars, writing and singing their own songs. A dog would be curled up nearby.

"It's just comfortable, peaceful in the wilderness," says Judy, who has created her own world in the large park, mixing her dreams and her imagination.

Beyond is a "museum" and then the burrow built into a hillside where she sleeps. Nearby she has a kind of shrine to "child existence. . .if you like kids and if you lost kids," says Judy softly. She says she was once married, and that her daughter was taken from her.

A twinkle in her eye, Judy shows her creative streak of humor as she explains a picnic basket set on a log. It is, she says with satisfaction, a wilderness joke.

"If a bear was to come in. . .you know how bears like to look at picnic baskets. . .and if I had any food in there, you could watch the bear open up the basket, take what he wants, leave casually, just leave you alone. Just watch the wilderness show."

Despite her cheerfulness, life in the park has not been easy for Judy, one of the thousands of homeless who would likely be diagnosed as mentally ill. Left to fend for herself, she has been the victim of rape and robbery. Roaming the park are teenagers who have attacked Judy, according to park rangers who keep an eye on her.

"I need humanity," says Judy. "I need rights in the courtroom. Protection. Relief. An apartment of my own. I wouldn't ask for no help."

Some of these homeless people are former patients in mental institutions who were discharged during the movement to deinstitutionalize the mentally ill in favor of treatment in community settings. In 1955, approximately 560,000 people lived in public mental hospitals. By 1980, there were only 120,000.

Two groups are heavily represented in that portion of the homeless population which is judged to be mentally ill—Vietnam veterans and single women without children.

This population has received increased attention as the public concern has grown, and politicians have taken some action. In New York City, Mayor Edward I. Koch announced that homeless who were deemed not able to take care of themselves would be involuntarily committed to hospitals. In the past, these homeless had to be literally endangering themselves to be taken off the streets. And provisions of the 1987 federal homeless assistance act will mete out more direct aid for the mentally ill homeless.

Critics says these efforts are too little, too political, and too shortsighted. The system has left the homeless adrift. One reason deinstitutionalization has backfired is that the money never followed the mentally ill out into the community as intended. Budget cutting has also had an impact.

A debate continues over whether deinstitutionalization is the wisest choice for the nation's mentally ill. Can the intensive programs needed to help these people be made available, and, in an age of massive spending cuts, how will such programs be funded? Can the current mental-health system, which many consider to be overly bureaucratic, be reformed?

If public officials, such as Mayor Koch, decide to pull the homeless off the street, will the system really be able to help them? Are there enough beds in hospitals? Will the homeless simply be ejected back out into the street, or will politicians also come up with the political will to provide long-term housing and services?

Community health centers that were supposed to deal with mental-health issues were not prepared to handle questions of housing, jobs, or training people to adapt to independent living. Though many people with mental problems successfully function on their own in society, those who can't are clustered in shelters, on the street, in train depots, libraries, and under bridges. They are often victims of crime, including robbery, assault, rape, and murder. Health care for simple problems such as colds or dental problems is nonexistent. These homeless suffer from circulatory diseases, malnutrition, and filthy living conditions. Time on the street often exacerbates paranoia.

Some shelters are able to employ trained mental-health workers. And when programs win the trust of the homeless mentally ill, they can in turn sometimes find housing with services for the mentally ill. But many smaller shelters, especially those run by nonprofit groups or churches, cannot maintain full-time workers in their facilities.

On a roadside near a highway in Memphis, Clarence thumbs through a stack of documents from his overflowing shopping cart. He says he can prove a judge is taking funds from his bank account. In a brisk winter wind, he pulls out a phone bill and compares it with a court date from another document. Clarence has circled numbers on the phone bill that match, though not in any sequence. He also has old bank statements with the same numbers circled randomly.

A tall, handsome, and polite Vietnam veteran who still wears his dog tags, Clarence says he misses his family, and waits to get back to them. A nearby homeless counseling center, which would be able to refer Clarence to mental-health treatment, has a three-by-five card with his name on it in their files. He had stopped in three months earlier, and the note said Clarence would come back a week later. He did not. He says most shelters and the Veterans Administration are not really a help. Many take money from contributors and pocket it, he says.

Dr. Farr sees the problem of the chronically mentally ill as a national emergency. He says the mental-health system needs to deal with the issue on three levels: emergency health care on the streets and in clinics; stabilizing care in which workers provide the mentally ill homeless with increased services and housing; and long-range planning to prevent future problems.

Still, many who see the mentally ill homeless, dressed in garbage bags or living on a grate, question how well this population can be served. Some argue that these people are being denied their rights by the very movement that claims it wants to help them. One reason for

deinstitutionalization was the horrendous conditions in some mental institutions.

But, in gaining their freedom, many of the homeless have ended up on the streets. Civil libertarians contend that even the chronically mentally ill know that shelters are unsafe, and that the answer is to reform the community response, not shove these citizens back into asylums.

Civil rights present a different question for the majority of homeless who are not mentally disabled. The loss of civil rights that befalls homeless Americans is a pervasive problem that must be addressed as squarely as the emergency need for food and shelter, say advocates for the homeless.

Incidents that would seem extraordinary to the average citizen are commonplace among homeless individuals and families.

When Joann and Richard invite a newspaper reporter to their motel in Poughkeepsie, they are threatened with eviction by the motel manager. A woman living in a New York City welfare hotel is described by the manager as "too vocal," and he asks his security guards to find a way to evict her.

At the end of the summer in 1987, a mother gets her children ready for the first day of school in the Los Angeles urban encampment in their dirt-floor tent next to a Cyclone fence. After a shower in the public bath, and brushing and rinsing their teeth with a garden hose as homeless alcoholics snore noisily nearby, the girls put on their clothes. One daughter puts on a pair of stockings with ragged runs. The new, donated shoes are a little too big, but the mother, an unemployed computer operator, stuffs newspaper into the toes.

Like children on the first day of school anywhere, the daughters pose with big smiles and bright eyes for their mother. Then they walk through the encampment, past still sleeping homeless adults, on their way to the school bus. Once on the bus, there is a delay. School officials had heard there were lice in the encampment, and there is some question whether these children—excited about the prospect of getting out of the camp to school—will be able to go to school. After discussion back and forth, and hours of delay, the children are finally sent to school, but not without confusion and dampening of their enthusiasm.

In suburban New York, some families want to enroll their children in schools near their "temporary" homes in motels, only to be told that the local school will not take the children. They must be sent over an hour each way—via taxi—to their previous schools. No matter that the average stay in the motel is a year. In 1987, suburban Westchester County spent $790,000 transporting homeless children to school.

"Homelessness in the United States is a massive assault on civil liberties," says John Hand of Westchester Legal Services in New York.

Mark, in his 30s, who lived in the urban encampment in Los Angeles, says it's almost an official attitude that the homeless have no rights.

"They've got the fences; they just need towers and guns and it would be a prison," says Mark. "It's a controlled environment. It's in the middle of nowhere, because they want you away from everybody, so you don't bother anyone, and so that. . . [the public] can't see the homeless. "I feel like a refugee in my own country," he says.

Some service-providers argue that persons in emergency shelter cannot be granted the same tenants' rights that people have in permanent housing. The tight control at the larger shelters is necessary for safety, they say. And some homeless agree. There is, without a doubt, a lot of violence on the street and in larger shelters and welfare hotels.

Others argue that the answer is to address the problem of the lack of affordable housing, rather than warehousing the homeless in the dangerous shelters. As shelters become the accepted low-income housing of the future, the loss of rights will become permanent for persons living in them.

Mr. Hand says there is a dilemma in the whole concept of emergency housing. He understands the need to get people into a shelter and to give them food, but money is being spent to build an institution that deprives people of their normal rights.

Since the fifties and sixties, important legal cases have given the poor stronger consumer, housing, and civil rights. For example, in the past tenants could be evicted from public housing without due process.

"Now we are seeing the same problems crop up in the context of emergency housing," says Hand. "But it is in a context that favors the government under the rubric of 'emergency.' "

"For those unlucky enough to be homeless, they are in a state similar to martial law," says Hand. "The new 'public housing' is sweeping away hard-fought rights."

Hand says he often tries to settle cases rather than take them all the way to court.

"Life is not that simple," says Hand, saying a family may prefer a less than satisfactory situation simply because it offers stability. "It's a multifaceted thing. Sometimes we want the easy remedy of a class-action suit. But if we oversimplify, we can hurt people."

"As advocates, we are sometimes risking the safety of our clients by advocating for them," say Beth Gorrie of the Coalition for the Homeless in New York City. She says sometimes the homeless don't know their rights, but often they do, and they still find themselves "out in the streets with their rights on."

She cites many cases of illegal evictions, sexual harassment, and physical and mental terrorism.

The acceptance of this "lesser citizenship" for the homeless is a classic example of blaming the victim, says Ms. Gorrie. Many homeless persons were evicted illegally, or lost their homes because the rent outstripped their ability to pay.

"They are put into the almshouse and then blamed," says Gorrie. "It's a frustration that we are talking in cliches; these stories are age-old."

take enormous political will and not a small amount of resources. At a time when housing experts are questioning how to allocate scarce resources—to the poorest of the poor, or spread out among the very poor, the working poor, and the middle class—the prospect seems daunting. An estimated 25 percent of the American public cannot find safe, decent housing at affordable prices. The poorer a household, the higher the percentage of its income is spent on housing.

There are some deep questions that should be asked about who the homeless are. Why has there been such an influx of young, single minority men? How come women and children are falling through the cracks so rapidly? What effect have cuts in federal programs had, and how has the current welfare system exacerbated the problems these families face? When nearly half of the homeless children in New York City do not attend school regularly, what sort of future will be theirs?

Certainly part of the solution, perhaps the most important part, must be our willingness to see the homeless as we see ourselves, not as an amorphous "them" that lives on the fringes of society waiting for a handout. Indeed, many advocates say that the quick fix of giving the homeless a quarter or even a dollar is often a way of buying off responsibility. There is usually no human contact between donor and recipient. Instead of communication there is distancing and even a deadening of the humanity of both participants. The country is helping and hating the homeless at the same time, they say.

The homeless are not necessarily heroes and not always victims. But for them the bottom has dropped out. And when we look in their faces we face the reality of loss—the loss of home, family ties, civil rights, self-esteem, opportunity, and the respect and acceptance of fellow citizens.

The problem of homelessness isn't easy to solve. The many contributing factors and the conflicting opinions of experts seem to have us in a state of confusion, both moral and otherwise. But in the end we must solve it and how we do that will have a lot to say about how we and the world view us as Americans.

Chantisse at the Prince George Hotel.
New York, New York

Above:
Outside Bloomingdale's.
New York, New York

Below:
Christmas, 1985, The Bronx.
New York, New York

Opposite:
A Prince George Hotel
resident, dislocated by a fire
on the eleventh floor,
comforts her daughter. A
child died in the fire.
New York, New York

Overleaf:
Sleeping on 28th Street after
the Prince George Hotel
fire.
New York, New York

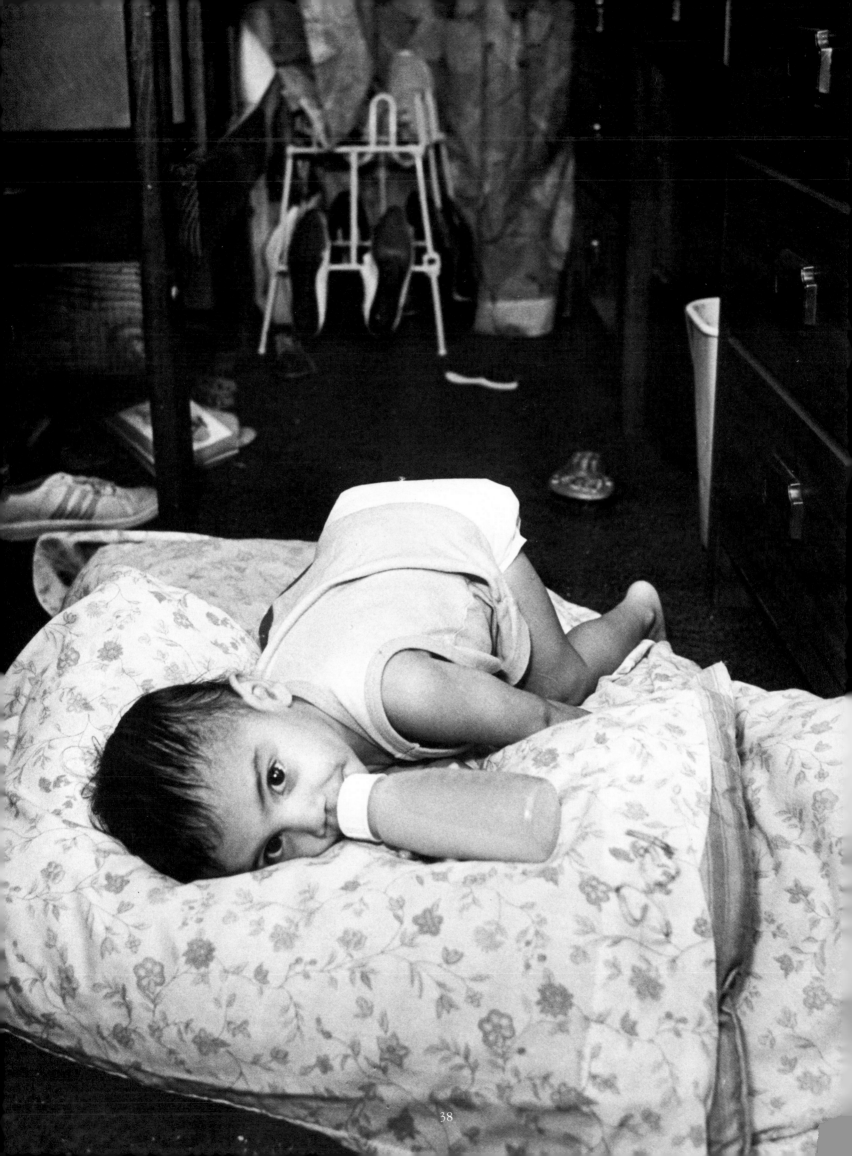

Opposite:
This is the only floor space
available in Junior's family's
$1,800 a month single room
at the Prince George Hotel.
His bottles are warmed over
an illegal hotplate which is
hidden when security guards
drop in. A New York
Health Department study
found that 18% of babies
born to homeless women in
hotels are of low birth
weight—under 5.5 pounds—
more than twice the 8.5%
figure for the city as a
whole.
New York, New York

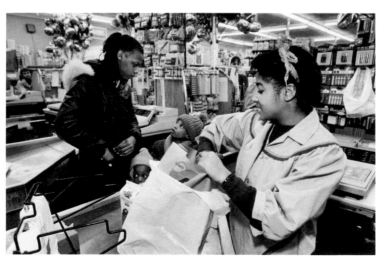

This page:
For almost two years,
Audrey and her three
daughters lived in a 20 by 10
foot room in New York's
Prince George Hotel. The
city paid the hotel owners
$1,668 a month to house
Audrey and her family. Now
in public housing, Audrey's
family is one of the lucky
few. Other low-income
families are unable to find
affordable housing. Their
numbers increased from 8.9
million in 1974 to 11.9
million in 1983, and
continue to grow.
New York, New York

This page:
Junior and his sister in the hallway of the Prince George, the only place in the hotel she can play after school.
New York, New York

Opposite:
Audrey prepares the last of the tuna fish for her daughters. It's Friday and she has three dollars to get her through Tuesday. The girls are used to the peanut butter and cold cereal that will be their diet through the weekend.
New York, New York

Overleaf:
Ruby and family in their $1,800-a-month room at the Carter Hotel in Times Square.
New York, New York

Opposite:
Eleven P.M. at a church-operated Emergency Assistance Unit on Church Street in Manhattan. A mother completes paperwork that may lead to shelter placement for the night. Sometimes the wait can last until the early hours of the morning.
New York, New York

Overleaves:
The Roberto Clemente State Park's gymnasium served as a shelter for families until it was closed as a health and fire hazard. Families lived in clumps of beds in the large open space, their belongings beside them. Advocate groups press for better alternatives such as rehabilitation of abandoned buildings and seizure of welfare hotels so that non-profit groups can run them.
New York, New York

This page:
For these young residents of the Prince George, telephone books in the hotel lobby are the chief entertainment. Trading back and forth, they throw each other names to look up. Jones, Roberts and Smith are easy. Robinson and Cleveland are stumpers.
New York, New York

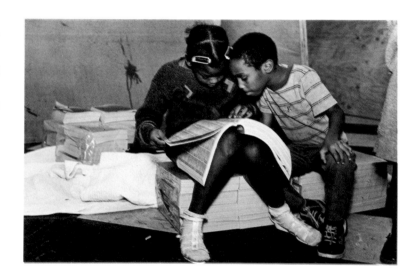

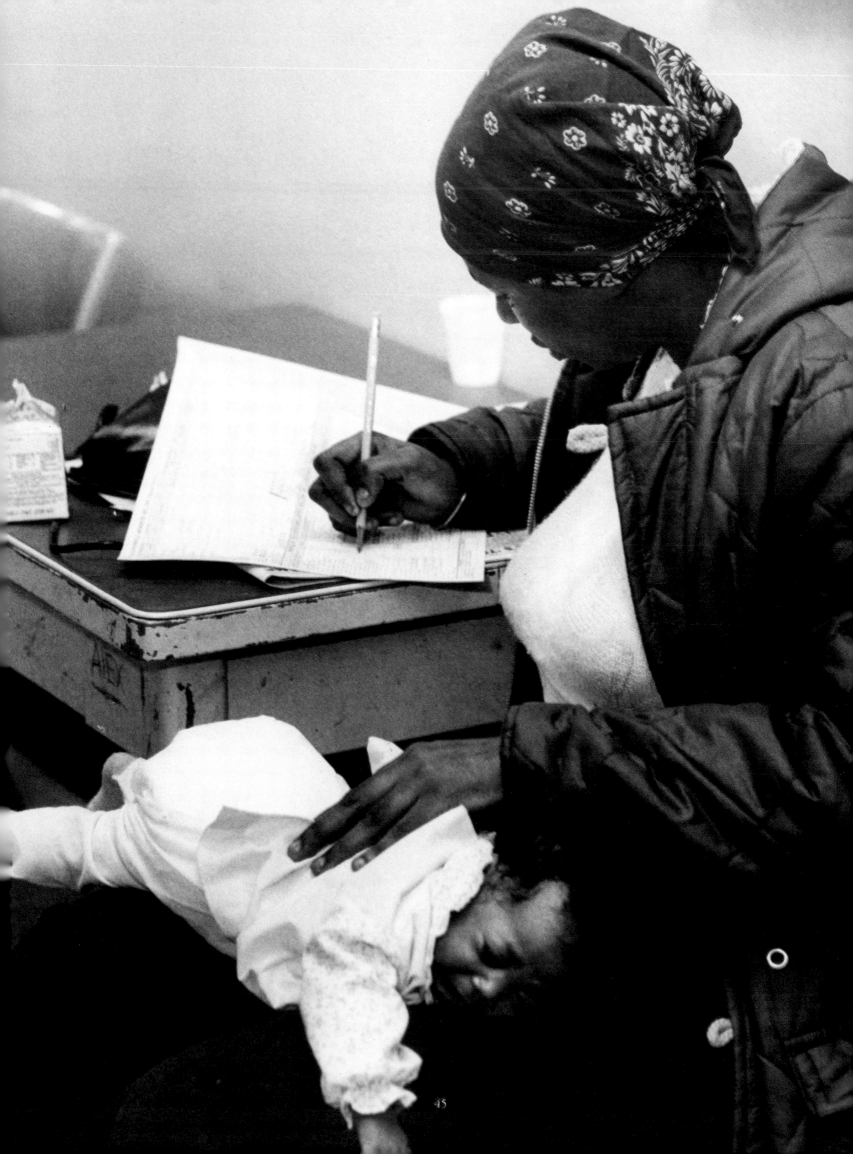

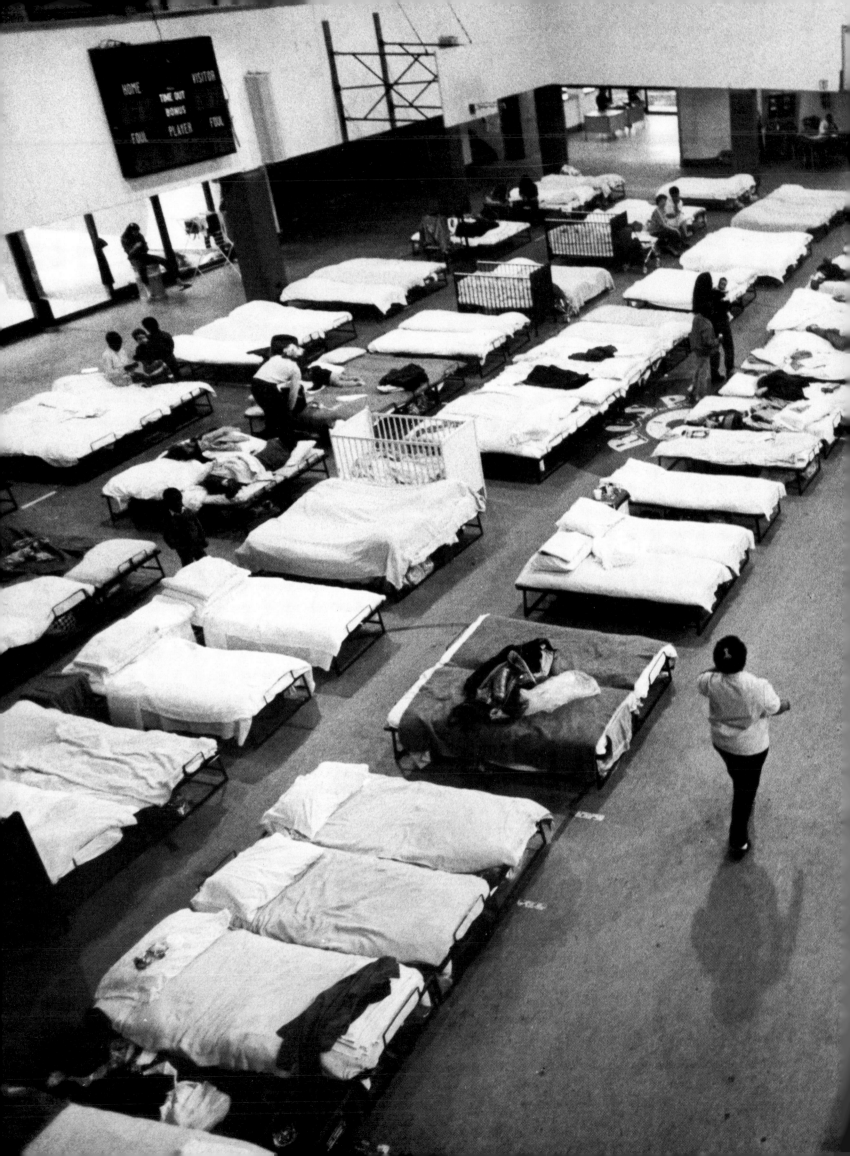

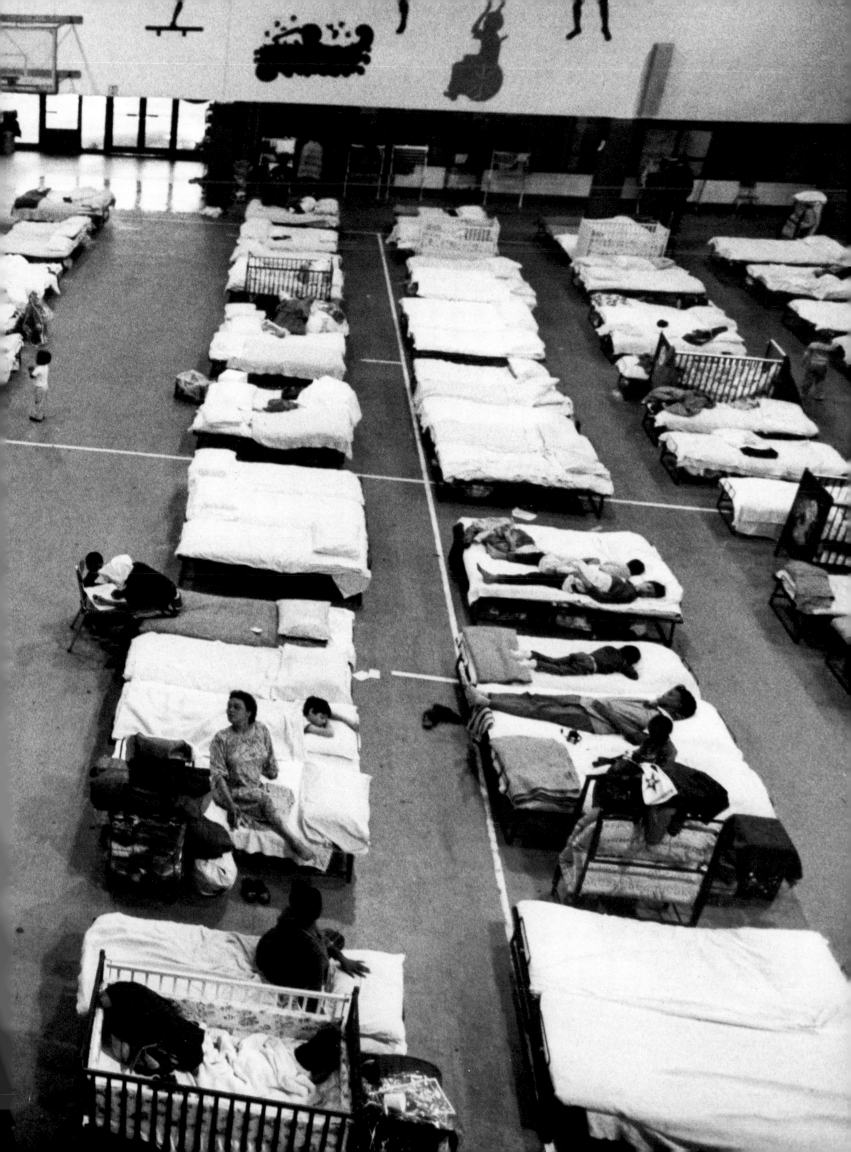

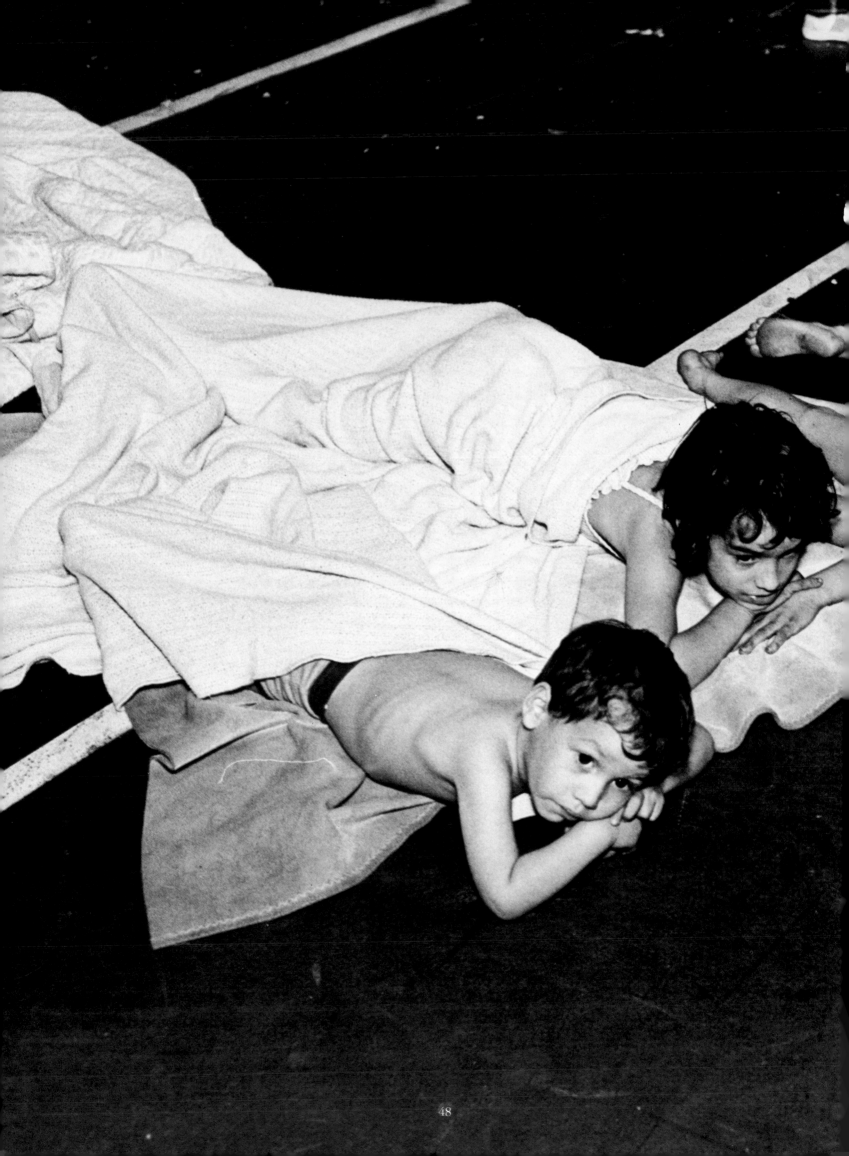

Thirty percent of America's homeless are Vietnam vets, some of them "conditionally anguished." Standing on the steps of the Capitol is the leadership of the newly-formed D.C. Homeless Vets. Washington, D.C.

This page:
Three homeless veterans in
front of Washington's
Vietnam War Memorial.
Washington, D.C.

Overleaf:
A homeless vet who prefers
to sleep on this marble
bench near the Reflecting
Pool, where he says police
patrols make him feel safer
than he does in the men's
shelter where he was
attacked.
Washington, D.C.

Opposite:
On the street.
Nashville, Tennessee

This page:
Shanty on the banks of the
Cumberland River.
Nashville, Tennessee

Overleaf:
Under a highway overpass
in Nashville, Dorothy sits in
her car wedged-in between
blankets, pots and pans.
She's in her sixties; she and
her husband, Tommy, have
been on the road a week.
Last night they slept in a
park. Tommy, a laid-off
carpenter, worries about his
wife's safety. "If I don't find
work here, I really don't
know what I'll do, 'cause
we're barely making it.
Working in the labor pools
for $3.35 an hour, I can't
even get ahead enough to
get an apartment to get my
wife off the ground."
Nashville, Tennessee

Terri smokes a cigarette underneath the
Victoria Memorial Bridge in Nashville.
Daughter of an Atlanta office manager, she's
been on the road since she left home at
nineteen.
Nashville, Tennessee

DAILY PUBLIC PARKING
PERMITTED IN THIS AREA
NO OVERNIGHT PARKING,
CAMPING, OR LOITERING
ALLOWED

TENN. DEPT. OF
TRANSPORTATION

POSTED
NO TRESPASSING
KEEP OUT

62

Opposite, this page, overleaf:
Thelma Marie lives in this school bus parked 20 feet from the road. She moved in several months ago when she couldn't pay the rent on her nearby home. Thelma works for the owner of the bus in exchange for meals and rent. A small coal stove heats the bus in winter. She lives on the $81 a month she gets from food stamps, and whatever else she earns from selling matchstick crucifixes she makes, and ginseng that she gathers in the hills with her friend. Thelma has two married daughters, one nearby and one in Maryland. Her four sons now live with their father in Florida, at her request. The state threatened to take them from her because she couldn't keep them off the road. She visited them four months ago. "I couldn't believe how they've grown. They wanted to come home with me. The baby was asleep when I left. I couldn't have woken him up. It would have killed me." Thelma says she's waiting for low income housing in Jonesville and that the Housing Authority has stopped taking applications. "They say they're that many up ahead of me, I'd have to wait more than likely ten years or longer." Watering her plants that survived the move she says, "Live or die." As for herself, "All I can do is take one day at a time." Pennington Gap, Virginia

Big Stone Gap, Virginia

Big Stone Gap, Virginia

Opposite:
A family's belongings.
Big Stone Gap, Virginia

This page:
This family stands in front
of the bus that sheltered
them last winter. Since then,
they've moved to temporary
housing, lacking heat and
running water.
Big Stone Gap, Virginia

Big Stone Gap, Virginia

Big Stone Gap, Virginia

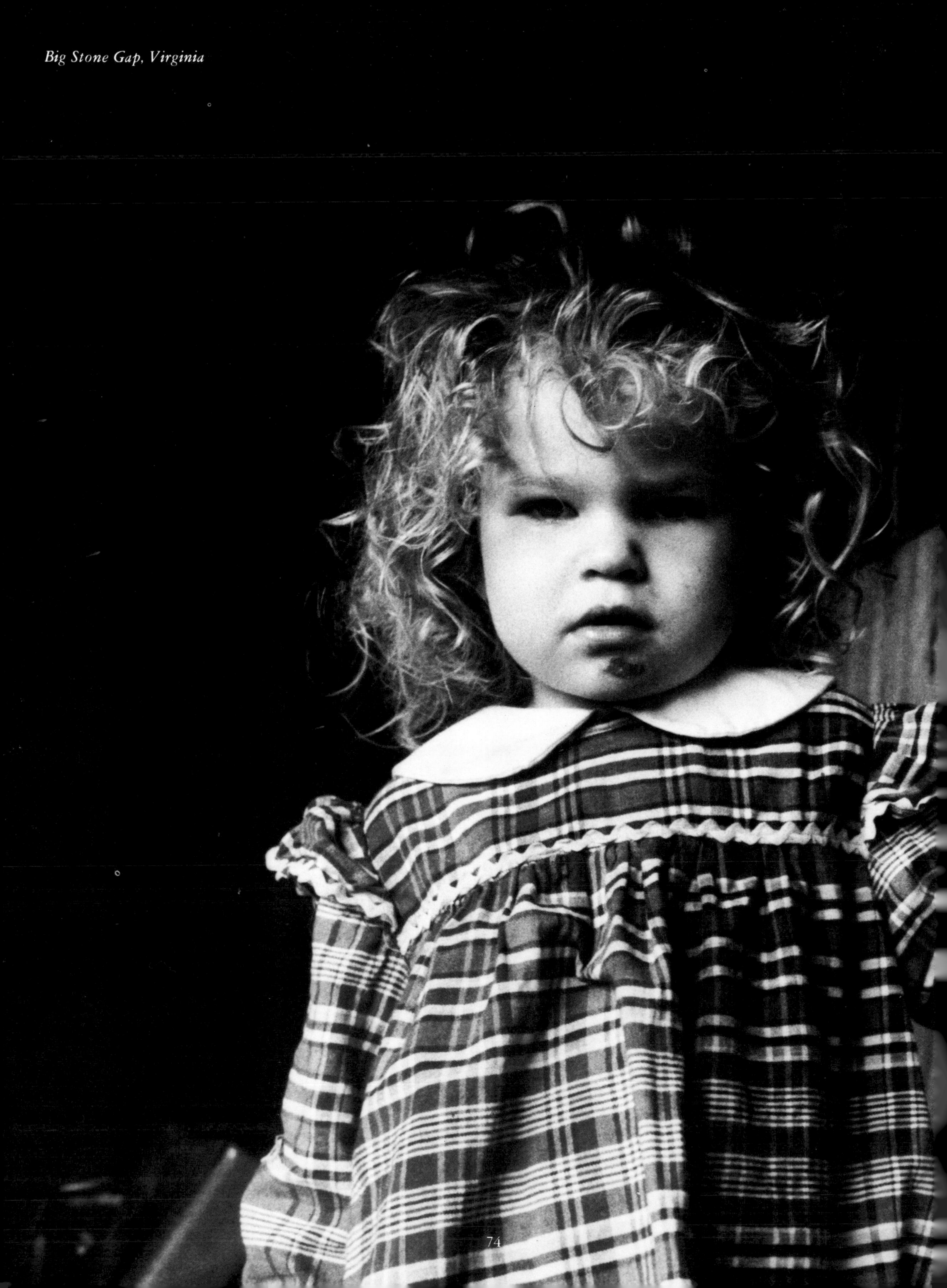

Jesse stops a minute to talk. He's been working on his stalled car parked in Tulsa's Salvation Army lot. "Here we are, we're just ourselves. We're not trying to be nobody. Wear no crown or nothing. No glory we don't deserve. We just want people to know that we are here, and we need help to get out of this mess. That's what America's all about. Or it was." Of a childhood that included illegitimacy, foster homes, truancy, drugs, and prostitution, he says, "I just really had a rotten start in life." He says he has been supporting himself since he dropped out of school in the sixth grade.

Jesse's wife Debra repacks the car out of which she and Jesse have lived on and off for several months. He says, "One of these days our boat's going to come in without a hole in it and we're going to make it. All I want in this world is a family and a job. That's it. Not much more you can ask for."
Tulsa, Oklahoma

Opposite:
Roberta Ann in the kitchen
of the Des Moines Catholic
Workers House where she
often eats.
Des Moines, Iowa

Overleaf:
Bobbie sitting in Tulsa
County's Emergency Shelter.
Tulsa, Oklahoma

This page:
Off of Tulsa's Highway 51,
Mike rests after changing a
tire. "Most of our valuables
are in our car. We had an
apartment. Work slowed
down, and we couldn't
afford to pay rent. I'm in
construction and when
construction's down, money
stops coming in."
Tulsa, Oklahoma

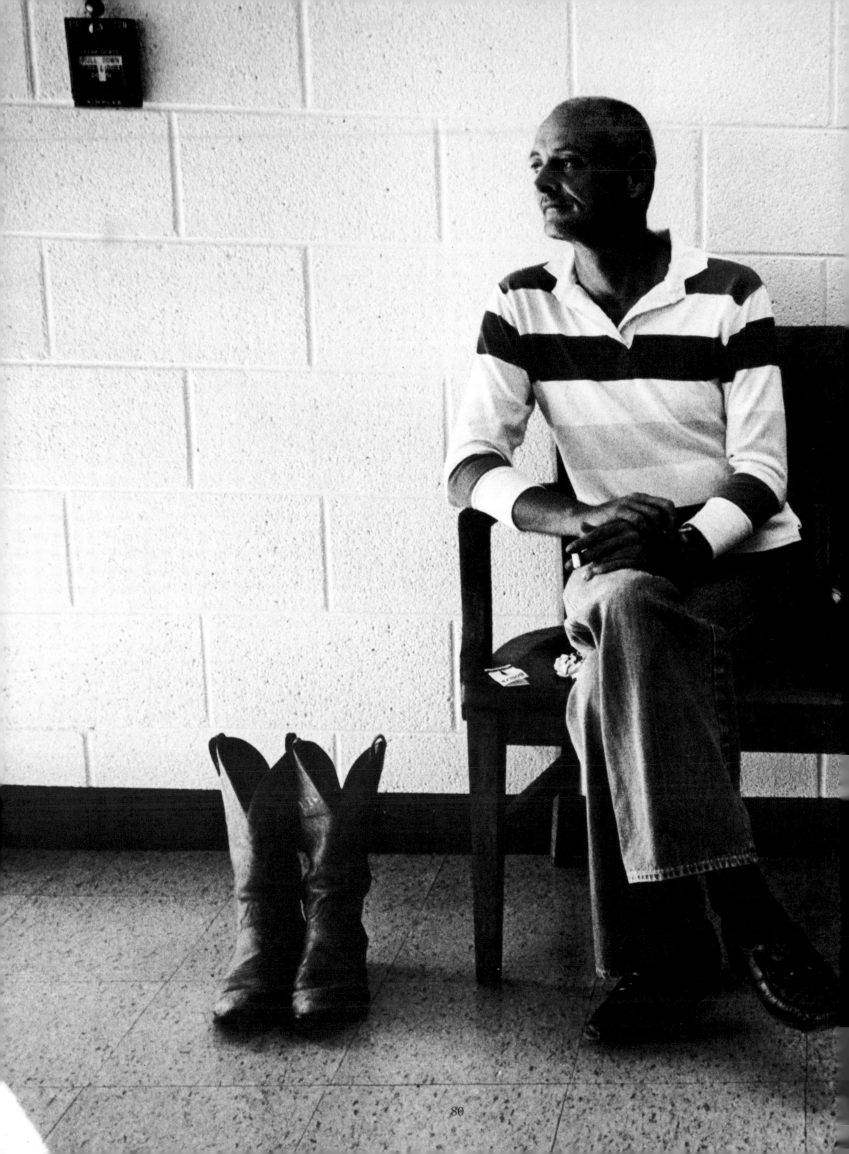

Originally Purchased
for the
Tulsa County Courthouse
6th & Boulder
1910-1954
Refinished & Identified October 1977

Dee, a dog groomer, says she lost her business when her Oklahoma clients started to lose their jobs in the oil slump. In her thirties, she is rail-thin and has not yet begun receiving public assistance. She was evicted from her trailer home when she couldn't make the payments on the mortgage. She and her son had no choice but to move in with her mother. A few days' stay turned into three months. "At least we have a roof over our heads," she says. "They did mention some possibility of getting some new job skills, which would be good because I need it. I have a high school diploma. That's not worth anything anymore.

"There needs to be something done. To me people are hurting too badly."
Tulsa, Oklahoma

Technically speaking, some homeless have a place to stay. Herbert, an elderly man in Milwaukee, lives in a roach-infested "furnished" room with one soiled mattress. He uses two rumpled jackets for a pillow and blanket. The linen he was promised when he paid the $120-a-month rent never appeared. He is hoping to get into Senior Citizen housing. Milwaukee, Wisconsin

This page:
The rules posted in this
shelter indicate that violence
can be the result of frayed
nerves and frustration.
Often families, the
chronically mentally ill,
veterans, and substance
abusers live side by side.
Milwaukee, Wisconsin

Overleaf:
Sister Connie Driscoll's
shelter for 130 women and
children.
Chicago, Illinois

88

Previous page, opposite, this page:
John and his family live in a substandard trailer in Key West's Pearl Trailer Court. John earns $12,000 a year as a diver and can't afford any more rent than what he is paying. They are just about to go to church. John has mounted an anti-drug campaign within the trailer park.
Key West, Florida

Overleaf:
In the parking lot of Miami's Salvation Army Shelter, Joylene and her family face the day. She has no money for transportation so her son carries the family's belongings in a plastic bag. In Miami there are only 695 beds for an estimated 8,000 who cannot find affordable housing. There is a waiting list of 15,000 for Miami's 6,000 public housing units. The wait can last for 25 years.
Miami, Florida

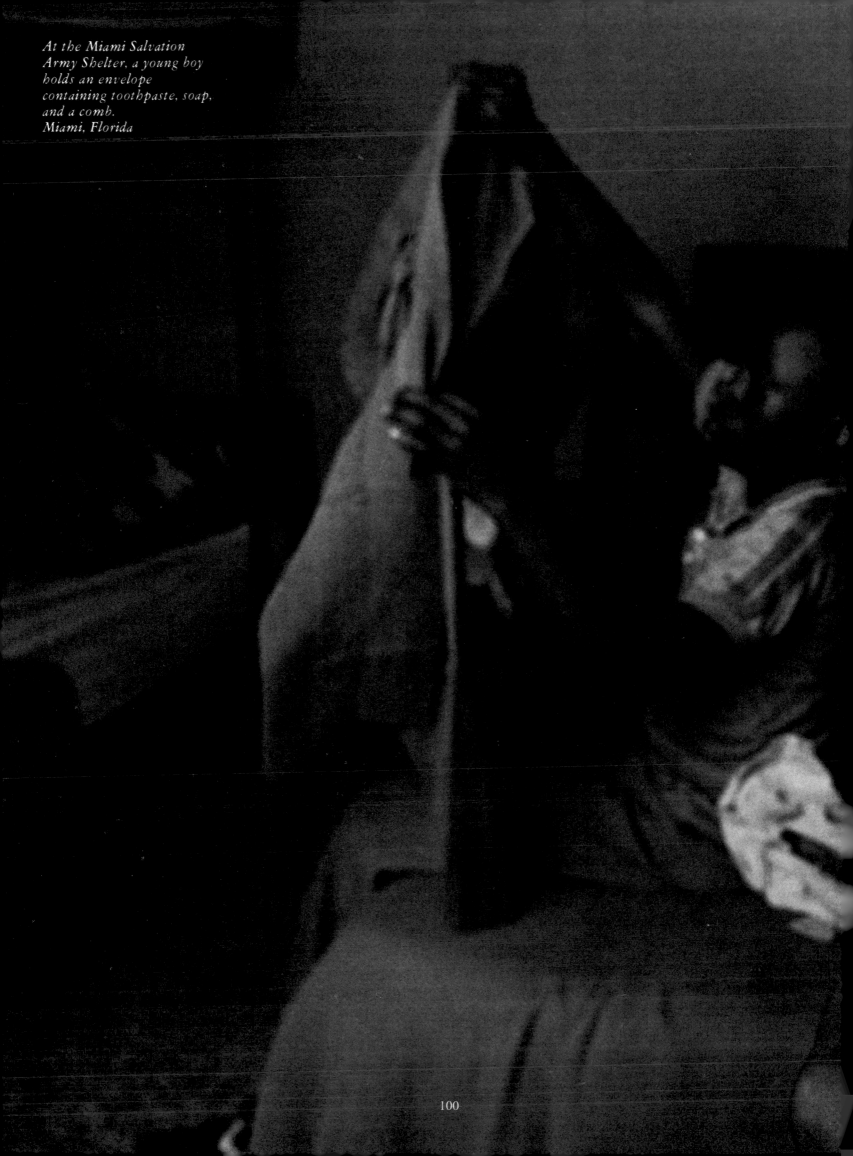

At the Miami Salvation
Army Shelter, a young boy
holds an envelope
containing toothpaste, soap,
and a comb.
Miami, Florida

Miami Salvation Army
Shelter.
Miami, Florida

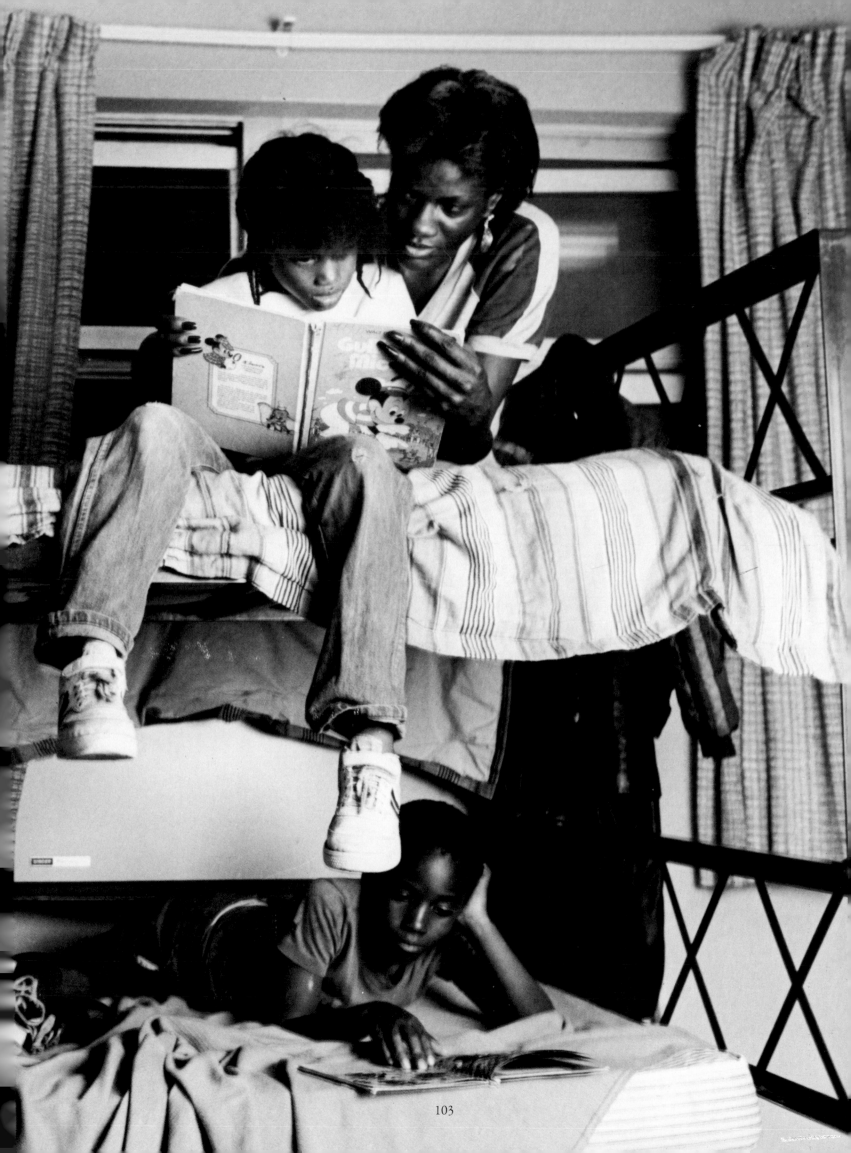

This page, opposite:
Ramshackle trailers, broken
glass from windows, and
trash mark this hidden
squatter community
surrounded by high-rent
areas. These young residents
live with their family in a
deserted cinderblock
building. Out of work
because of a bad hip, their
father wired in electrity
from a neighbor's trailer.

The family station wagon
sits in the driveway stuffed
with the family's belongings.
Key Largo, Florida

Key Largo, Florida

*Children ___ ___ cans they
collected ___ income.
Coahoma, Mississippi*

*A Coahoma mother
describes the day the
community first cleared the
lot on which the new homes
would be built: "We got up
one Saturday morning
around eight o'clock, me and
50 little kids, and started
clearing it off. We were*

*throwing bricks and trash ___
around. We didn't even yet
know how to stack bricks,
you know, but we were
trying."
Coahoma, Mississippi*

This page, above:
Leo, Coahoma resident and
volunteer, nails in siding for
one of his community's new
houses.
Coahoma, Mississippi

This page, below:
Coahoma children sweep the
floor and mix compound,
helping to build their new
house.
Coahoma, Mississippi

Previous page:
Four children sleep on the
only bed while their mother,
Catherine, sleeps on a cot in
the kitchen. Catherine's
brother, who works at night,
often drops off his children
for the night. Catherine
says, "I take one mattress off
the bed and put it on the
floor and leave the rest on
the bed's box. Then the
couch is full and the floor is
full. We manage. It's kind of
crowded but we have
sleeping room at least. Just
don't knock on the door and
expect to walk right in
because you're likely to step
on someone's head."
Coahoma, Mississippi

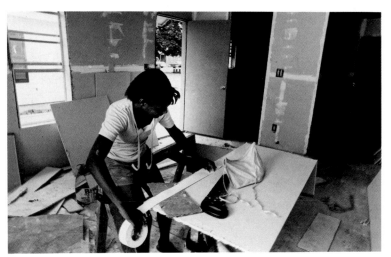

This page:
Habitat volunteers pose
with Ray Hunt, right,
former ITT executive now
working with Habitat For
Humanity. Hunt says,
"There are quite a few
people in this town who live
on $155 a month income
plus food stamps. That's a
single parent, most likely.
There's 75-80%
unemployment here, too."

"Our primary focus here...
has been providing
inexpensive housing. We're
looking at 50 to 60 dollars a
month being the maximum
payment. You get the
payment much above that
here and you're going to
disqualify a large portion of
the town. It looks like our
first three bedroom house
we're building for $7,500
approximately. And our first
four-bedroom house for
$8,200. Bear in mind there's
no labor cost and we've
shopped hard for the
materials. But these are
houses that have been
specifically designed for low-
cost by an architect. They
meet HUD minimum
poverty specifications."
Coahoma, Mississippi

Overleaf:
Velma and her family in
front of the house which her
Habitat house will replace.
Coahoma, Mississippi

Opposite and overleaf:
In Atlanta's Cabbagetown an eviction is in
progress, not uncommon in this gentrifying
neighborhood. Eighteen-year-old Gwendolyn
stands in the yard guarding her family's
belongings, which were put out that morning.
They were two months behind in their rent
payments. "They're good folks," said the local
policeman. Gwendolyn earns $3.75 an hour
working at a local fast-food restaurant.
Atlanta, Georgia

Ron and his family in Denver's Samaritan Shelter. "You lose your job and everything you own goes back.... I was working in a faucet company in Oklahoma. We got paid pretty good. One day I lost my job. The next day people found out and sent people out to make sure I could still make my payments. Of course I couldn't, so everything went back.

"One day you have your friends over cooking steak on the grill. The very next weekend, you find yourself loading up the car, having to leave clothes behind. All of our personal belongings we had to give away or sell, or leave, because we couldn't carry them in the car. Most we'll never see again.

"I now work as a security guard for $4.00 an hour. Most people want you to come down with $500 or $600 to rent a house. That's a lot of money to come up with at $4.00 an hour. It takes you a month to come up with your money for deposit. You have to pay deposit on the gas bill and electric bill. We have to get our daughter's clothes at Goodwill."
Denver, Colorado

Homeless family under a
highway overpass near Salt
Lake City's family shelter.
Salt Lake City, Utah

*This page, opposite:
Katherine Ann, her husband
and their daughter were on
their way to Florida
relatives, when their car
broke down. A Mormon
elder sent them to Travelers
Aid where their request for
bus tickets to Florida was
turned down when no one
answered at the Florida
number. With vouchers for
diapers and a night's
lodging, they were back on
the street.*

*The selection of information
pamphlets at Travelers Aid
includes a flyer soliciting
plasma donors from the
transient and homeless who
pass through Salt Lake City.
Salt Lake City, Utah*

*Overleaf:
Waiting for a train out of
town.
Salt Lake City, Utah*

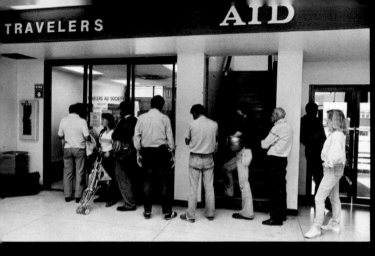

Opposite, below:
Located under a highway
overpass, Salt Lake City's
family shelter is isolated
from downtown Salt Lake
City. There are an estimated
500,000 homeless children
in America. According to
the National Conference of
Mayors, they are the fastest
growing segments of the
homeless population. The

shelter in Salt Lake City has
its own school, but most of
America's homeless live in
dehumanizing conditions,
unable to attend school for
transportation and
adminstrative reasons.
Salt Lake City, Utah

Previous page:
Playing in the parking lot of
the Salt Lake City family
shelter.
Salt Lake City, Utah

Underneath a highway overpass in Salt Lake City, a window cleaner named Thomas rests before catching a freight train out of town for Grand Junction. "I'm not going to get on that train sleepy and fall and kill myself," he says. "I've been on the road, it will be three years in November. I got divorced and the judge gave everything to her and I left with a pick-up truck and $3,000. I blew the money and wrecked the truck and I just wanted to get to the next town. A guy told me, 'Well, man, all you got to do is hop a freight.' I said, 'Well, how do you do it?' He said, 'I'll show you.,' I've been doing it ever since.
"If I knew how to catch a train to Denver, that's where I'd be because of window cleaning. They have so many high-rises there that there's lots of work. I believe I can get to Grand Junction."
Salt Lake City, Utah

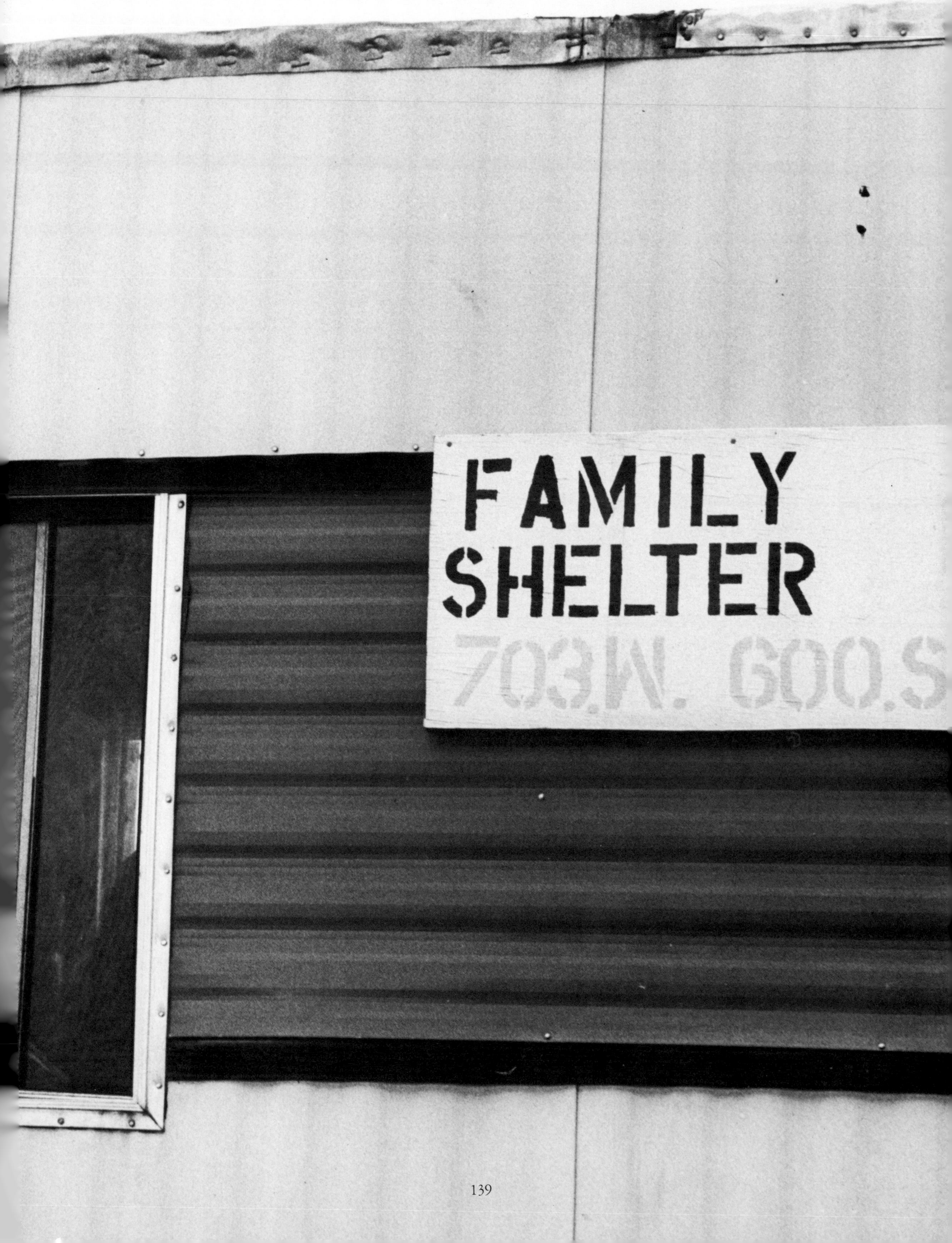
FAMILY
SHELTER
703.W. 600.S

On Route 40, New Mexico, Elma Jane waits
for a tow-truck to pull her car to a station. At
63 she lives on Social Security payments of
$290 a month and has been living out of her
car with her cats. She's headed for the east
coast if her car can make it. "It's a totally
different world from thirty years ago," she
says. "You could have your pick of four or five
jobs. You picked, they didn't pick you, and wait
two or three months to tell you. They were
delighted to have you and treated you well.
I found myself out of work, when I was fifty-
eight, I believe. That was when Mr. Reagan
pulled the funds out of my job. I was director
of two counties of Idaho Community Action
and also public relations for eight counties,
trying to promote community action programs
to the public, to make them aware and ask
their help as volunteers.
"As you get older,...[you find that] they want
the cute girls whether they have a brain in
their heads, or education or experience. It
makes no difference to most employers,
especially men employers. I'm not trying to be
mean. It's a fact. A woman gets to be fifty-five,
she's got a problem. Her education and
experience don't make a difference. She's going
to have difficulty getting a job."
Route 40, New Mexico

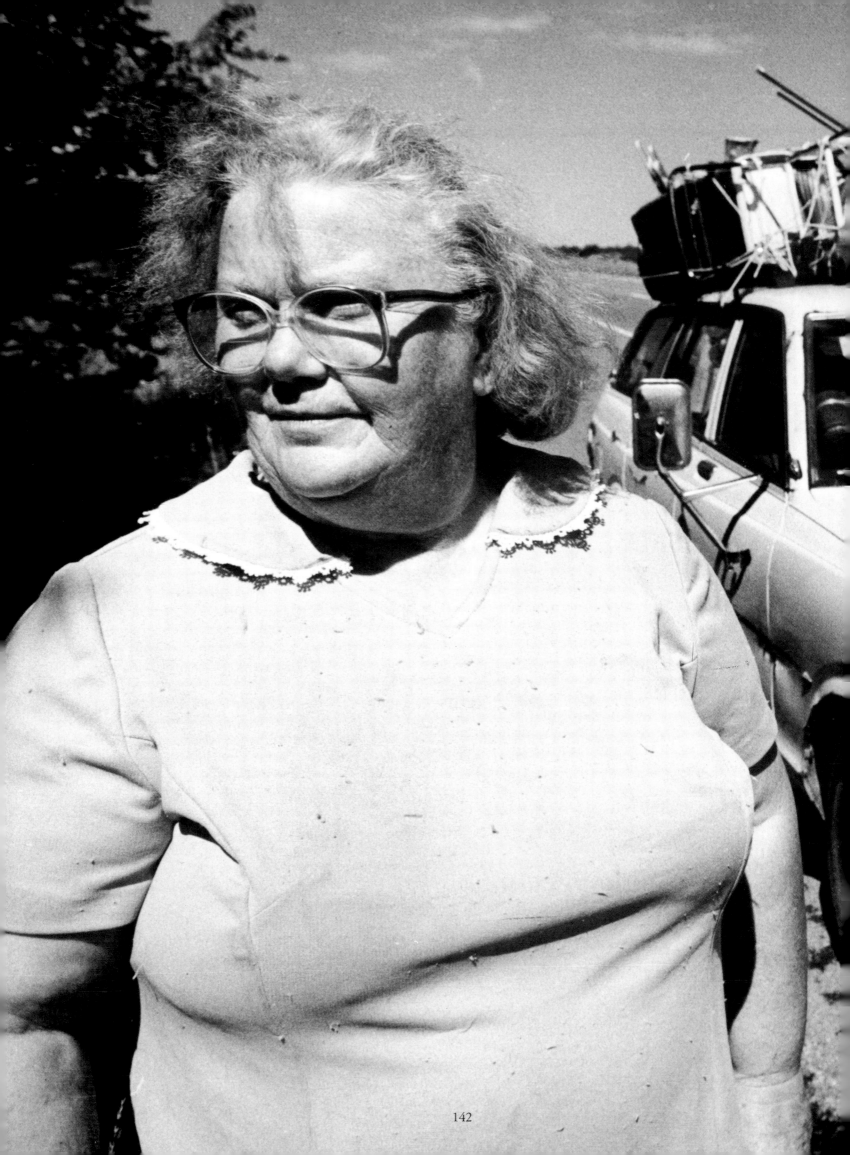

CHRIST IS THE ANSWER

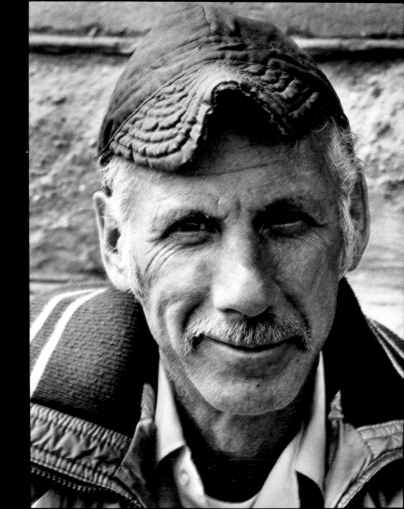

Previous page:
A family, outside of
Albuquerque.
Albuquerque, New Mexico

This page.

Florence holds her daughter Tina in her arms as her husband Roger hitches a ride for the family. They want to get back into town. They had to leave the shelter, six miles from town, at seven in the morning. Two nights earlier the family slept under a tree after Florence had gotten sick from the food in a women's shelter. Originally from Salt Lake City, Roger says he lost his job as a housepainter. They decided to go to Florence's mother in New Orleans, Louisiana. There they found they were crowding the others living there so they took to the road. Their car broke down in El Paso, Texas, and they had no money for repairs. They had to leave the car at the side of the road and hitched the way to Albuquerque. "I'm not used to this," says Florence grimly, after the family spent the night on the shelter's floor.
Albuquerque, New Mexico

Overleaf.
Homeless couple living out of their car in a "camp" near Albuquerque's railroad tracks.
Albuquerque, New Mexico

This page:
Richard, a union electrician
from Texas, came to
Albuquerque on the promise
of a job that fell through.
Now he works as a night
watchman for $3.35 an hour
and lives in a camper.
Albuquerque, New Mexico

Opposite:
Homeless "camp" in
Albuquerque. The residents
all look out for each other in
this high crime area near
the railroad tracks.
Albuquerque, New Mexico

Overleaf:
Jo Anne and her children
wait for her husband in
their car outside an
Albuquerque soup kitchen.
Albuquerque, New Mexico

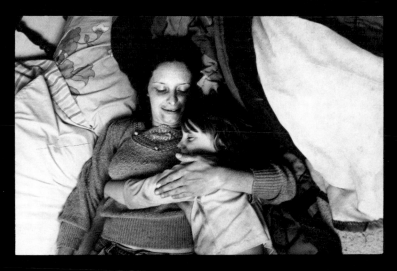

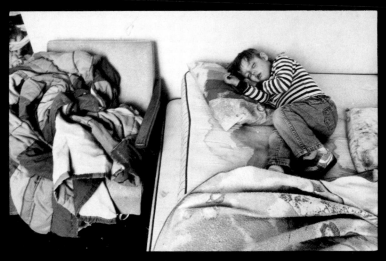

Previous page:
Homeless couple in their camp on the banks of the Rio Grande.
Albuquerque, New Mexico

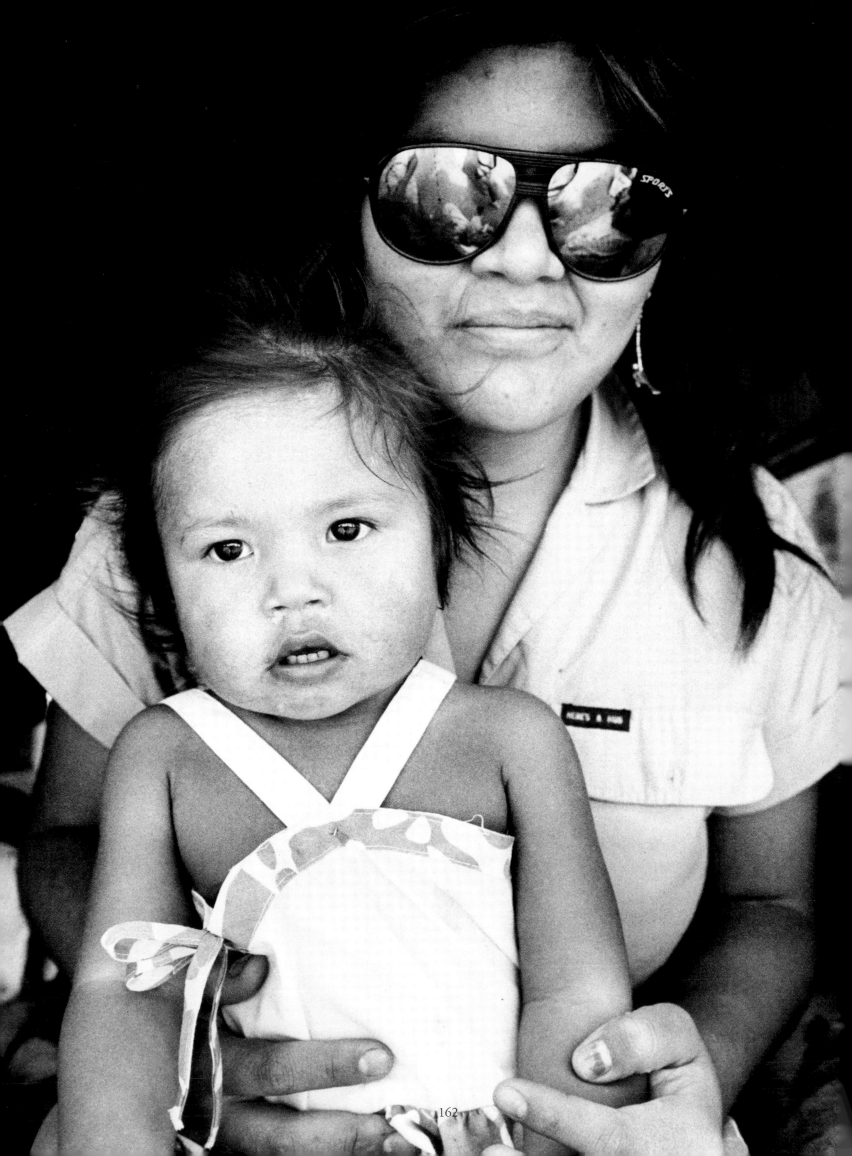

This page:
A land dispute between the
Navajo and Hopi tribes
froze ancestral Navajo lands
and made living there
illegal. Rose, a Navajo made
homeless by the dispute,
built this shelter on the land
in question.
Tuba City, Arizona

Overleaf:
Rose in front of her illegal
shelter.
Tuba City, Arizona

Previous page:
A Navajo mother and her son take a walk through the Navajo land where they once lived.
Keam's Canyon, Arizona

Opposite:
Picking wild herbs with her son, this Navajo woman said, "I think a lot of families broke up because of that [the land dispute], because they had to leave the reservation, their homes. You hear the phrase 'driven to drunkenness'. Well, a lot of people got that way, too. They just went on the road and they're down in Gallup, laying in the gutter because they lost their homes. That's what happens, I guess, when you take someone away from their home. It's sad."
Keam's Canyon, Arizona

This page:
These youngsters will not inherit their grandmother's land which was lost in the land dispute.
Keam's Canyon, Arizona

Overleaf:
Five generations of this family have lived on the land they had to relinquish in the Hopi-Navajo dispute. Now the tribe must pay rent to the Hopis so that the grandmother can remain until her death.
Keam's Canyon, Arizona

Homeless father and
daughter outside Salt Lake
the Star of Hope Mission
in Houston.
Houston, Texas

This page and opposite:
"You look at the Houston
Chronicle and there's lots of
jobs, but for every job
there's tons of people
applying. Even for a job
selling hotdogs in the
stadium. It's a mind-
scrambling situation to find
yourself homeless, to build
up the courage to be tough
and go out there and say,
'Hey, I'm not afraid of this.'"
Houston, Texas

Overleaf:
In the Salvation Army
Shelter parking lot it's safer
to play on the roof of the
car.
Houston, Texas

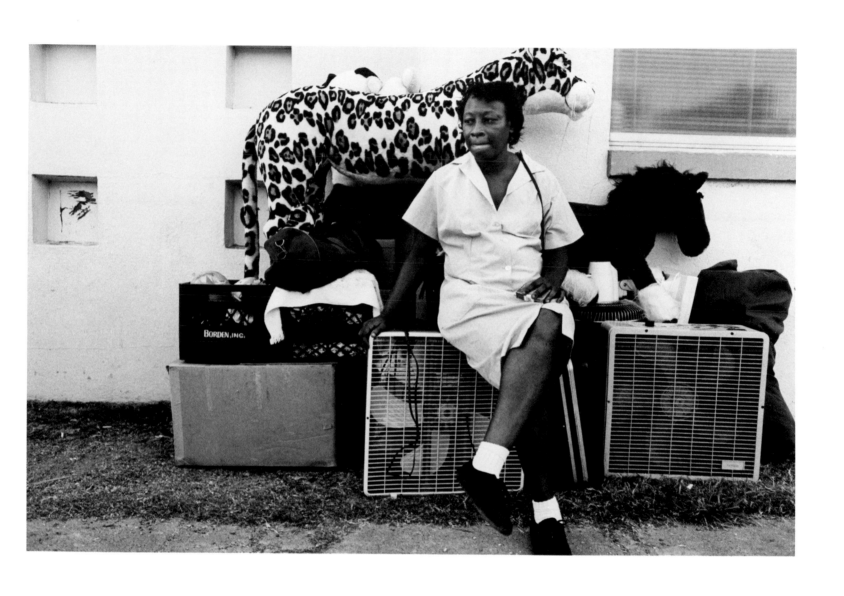

175

This page, above:
Young residents of the Star
of Hope Mission.
Houston, Texas

This page, below:
Grandmother with her
grandchildren at the Star
of Hope Mission.
Houston, Texas

This page, above:
Star of Hope Mission.
Houston, Texas

This page, below:
Star of Hope Mission.
Houston, Texas

Overleaf:
Star of Hope Mission.
Houston, Texas

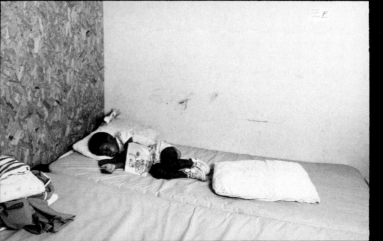

181

Opposite, and overleaf:
Late afternoon light glinted off the battered
Toyota pick-up truck on the side of Highway
40, ten miles outside of Amarillo, Texas. The
truck belongs to Elsie and her family, and it is
packed to the limit with a bed, a fan, and a
dresser.
Inside the cab Elsie sat between her two
grandchildren and her husband. They just
recently left Mississippi and were bound for
California. "There just wasn't anything left for
us in Mississippi," she offered when pressed.
She stared silently at the highway ahead, with
her grandson on her lap. "We just want to get
as far as Tecumcari tonight."
Amarillo, Texas

This page:
Many families from the
Phoenix area are forced to
live in the desert. The
homeless problem has
reached crisis proportions
there. The Salvation Army
Family Service Center say
they could easily average 125
families a night but there is
room for only twelve. By
June of 1986 they had
housed as many families as
they had in all of 1985.
Where do those who are
turned away find shelter?
Donna Skinner, Director of
the Service Center says, "I
guess they go to the river
bottom, stay in cars, camp or
just keep roaming about
town."
Apache Junction State Park,
Arizona

Overleaf:
Apache Junction State Park,
Arizona

189

Previous page:
Apache Junction State Park,
Arizona

This page:
Gaby, twelve, with her
brother and sister and a
neighboring camper's son.
She and her family of ten
members moved to the
desert after being evicted
from a hotel room. At this
time there were 100-200
people living in this desert
location. Michelle, Gaby's
mother, told a newspaper
reporter, "We were just
camping out at first. But
then we couldn't find
anything [a place to stay].
And when the crust under
your fingernails grows and
your hair is filthy and it's a
pain in the ass, it's not
camping anymore. It's not
camping when this is where
you live. When you can't go
home."
Apache Junction State Park,
Arizona

This page:
Gaby shoulders a great deal of the responsibility of her family's care. A recent Harvard study of homeless children found that rootless life can harm children. They discovered sleeping disorders, depression, and delayed developmental skills. The Phoenix Gazette reports that often homeless children are stung by the barbs of peers. Gaby's mother says schoolmates taunt her children with epithets like "dirt bag". Her ten-year-old daughter, Margaret, came back to camp one day in tears after some children passed a petition aimed at getting the "squatters" off the school bus.
Apache Junction State Park, Arizona

Overleaf:
Apache Junction State Park, Arizona

Apache Junction State Park,
Arizona

196

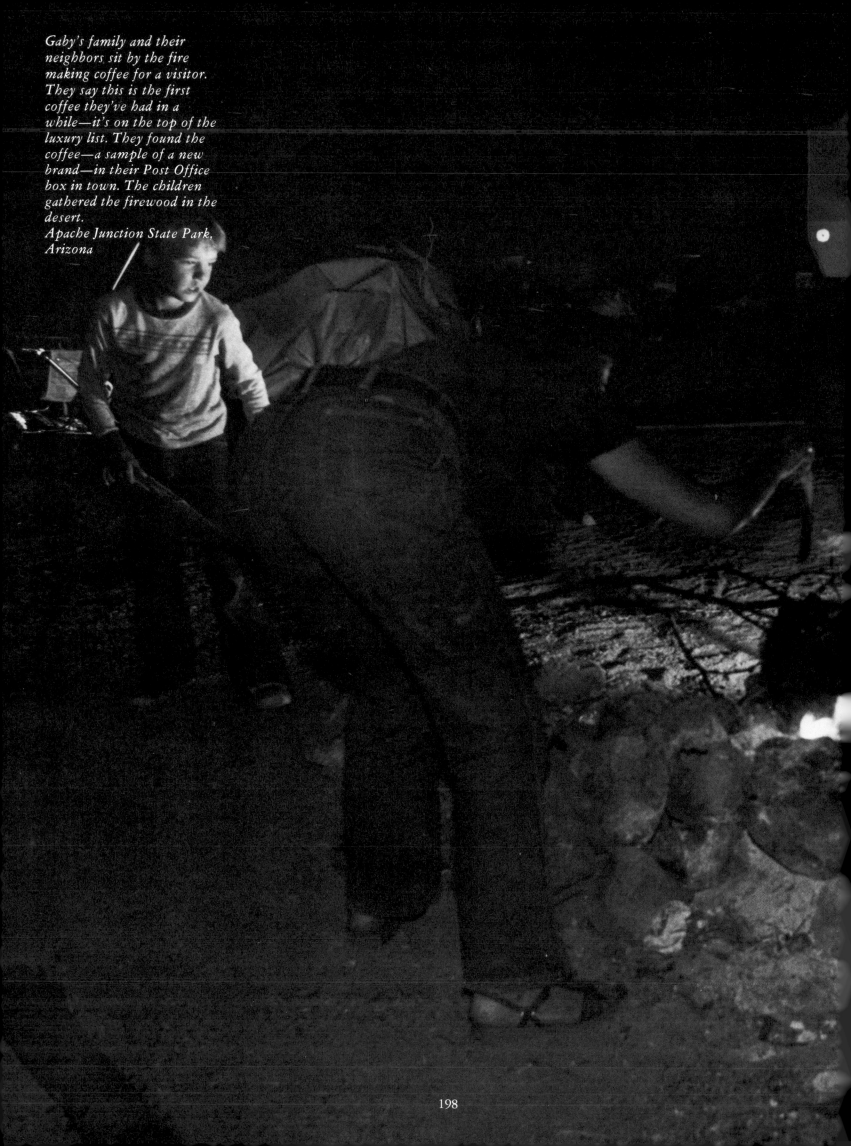

Gaby's family and their neighbors sit by the fire making coffee for a visitor. They say this is the first coffee they've had in a while—it's on the top of the luxury list. They found the coffee—a sample of a new brand—in their Post Office box in town. The children gathered the firewood in the desert.
Apache Junction State Park, Arizona

This page:
Pacific Palisades walkway
Santa Monica, California

Overleaf:
Venice, California

Griffith Park
Los Angeles, California

Judy lives in the hills of Griffith Park in Los Angeles in a camp she's constructed in the woods according to what she calls "show script." She protects herself by carrying a big stick and wears a dog-chain around her neck. She says she has been raped three times by "bushers"—transients that sleep in Griffith Park's bushes. Nevertheless, the world Judy has created is a gentle one where coyotes howl and imaginary friends visit her campfire to sing songs at night.
Los Angeles, California

Previous page:
"If I had my own apartment
I would leave the wilderness
in peace like I wasn't even
here".
Griffith Park
Los Angeles, California

This page:
Griffith Park.
Los Angeles, California

Opposite:
"I've been here ten months.
You dog it in and dog it out.
It's comfortable at night,
real comfortable".
Griffith Park
Los Angeles, California

Overleaf:
*Los Angeles urban
encampment.
Los Angeles, California*

*Previous page:
Los Angeles urban
encampment.
Los Angeles, California*

*This page:
Los Angeles urban
encampment.
Los Angeles, California*

*Opposite:
The urban encampment in
downtown Los Angeles was
a dirt lot surrounded by a
Cyclone fence. The 600
residents nicknamed it "The
Dustbowl Hilton." They
were frisked each time they
entered the camp and got
their running water from
garden hoses.
Los Angeles, California*

221

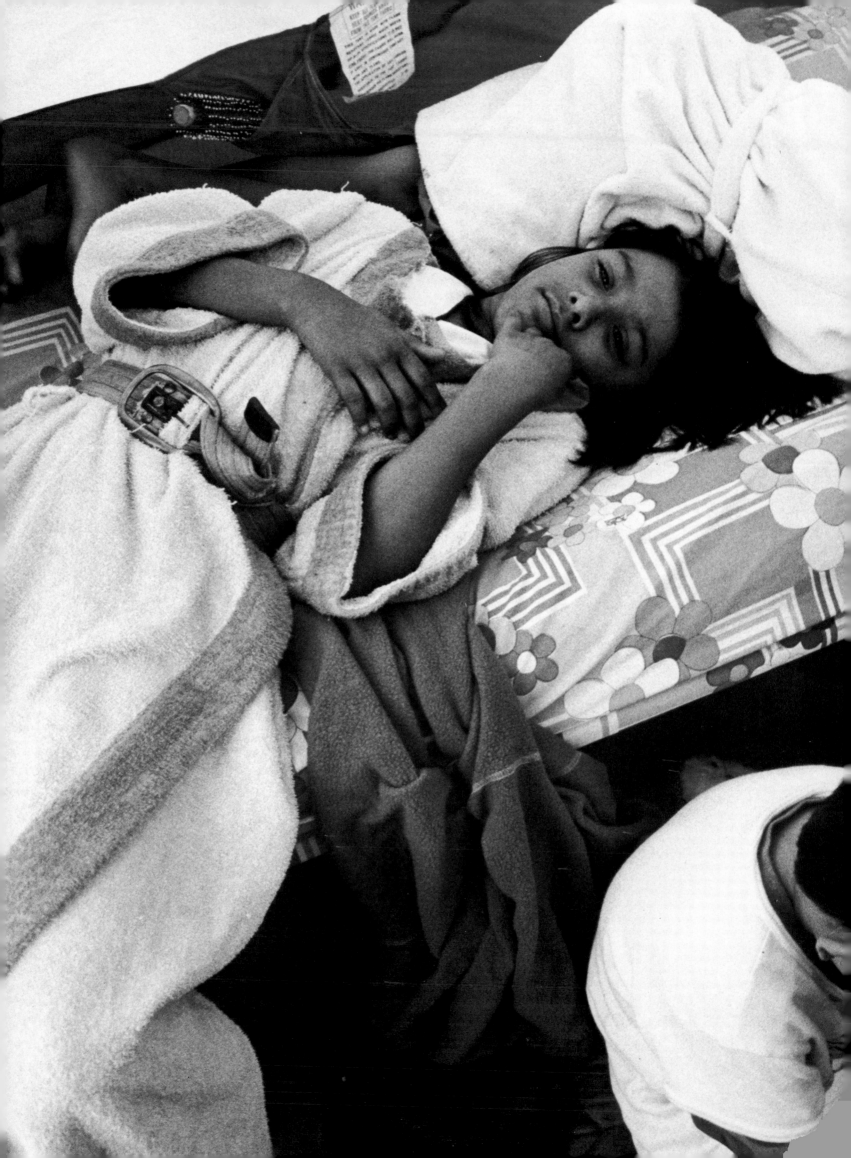

Below, top:
People living in their
vehicles created this camp,
nicknamed "Shabbytown."
Wilmington, California

Below, bottom:
Shabbytown.
Wilmington, California

Below, top:
Los Angeles urban
encampment.
Los Angeles, California

Below, bottom:
A plasma center in
downtown Los Angeles, the
chief source of income for
many homeless.
Los Angeles, California

Urban encampment resident
gets a free haircut from a
volunteer Los Angeles
hairdresser.
Los Angeles, California

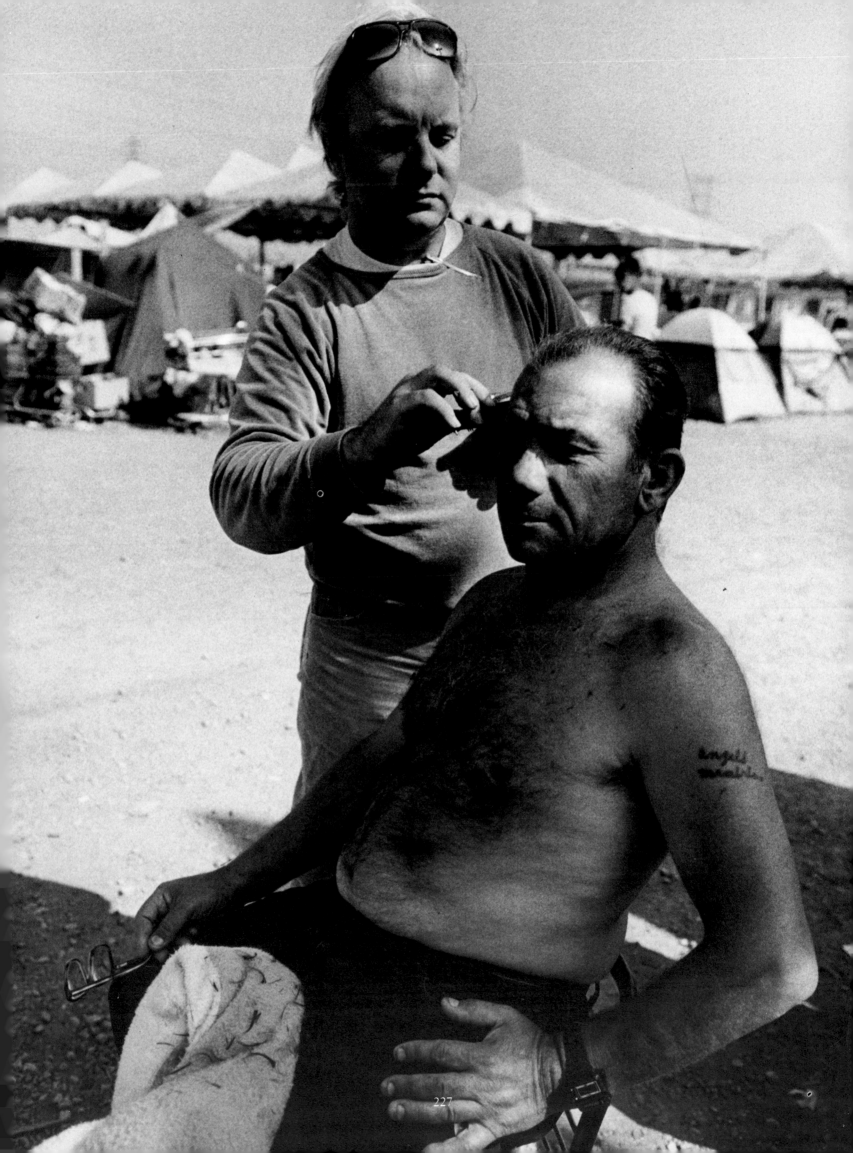

I can see the tears in the kids' eyes
I can feel the pain in their hearts
Sometimes it makes me fall apart
Because I am a man with a child's heart.

I look in their eyes it makes me want to cry
I see many things inside
I say to myself what are they doing here
I look into their eyes when they first arrive
And I can see the fear and hear their
Moms saying what am I doing here.

I still say to myself what are they doing here
My heart is strong I say to myself
Help them carry on, help them to be
*   themselves.*
So I be myself and act a fool
Just to make them feel approved.

Because there will never be a broken
child in my homeless school.
Yes a school of love, a school of pain,
we all must learn
we are the same.

So take my hand and walk with me
so our god can set us free.
Free from all the same we do
so we can help the homeless too.
I am a man with a child's heart.

A poem by Rufus H.,
urban encampment resident
Los Angeles, California

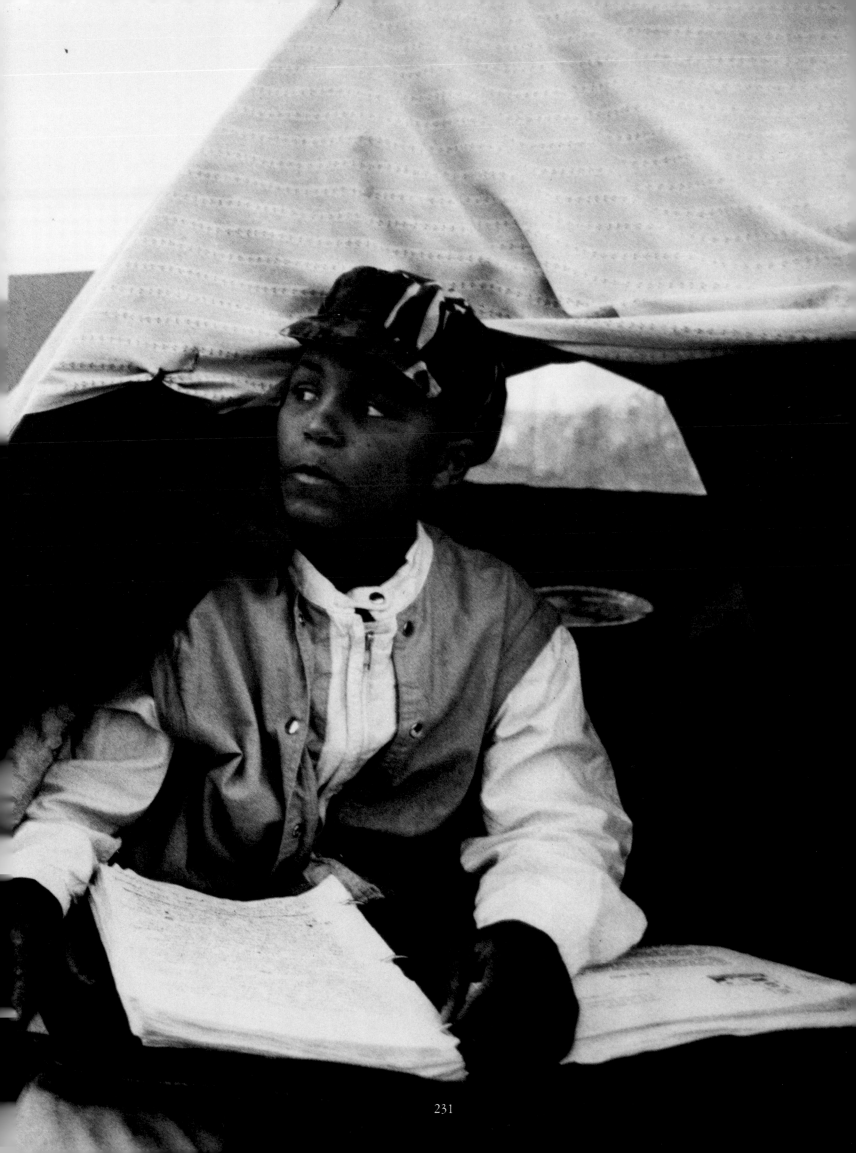

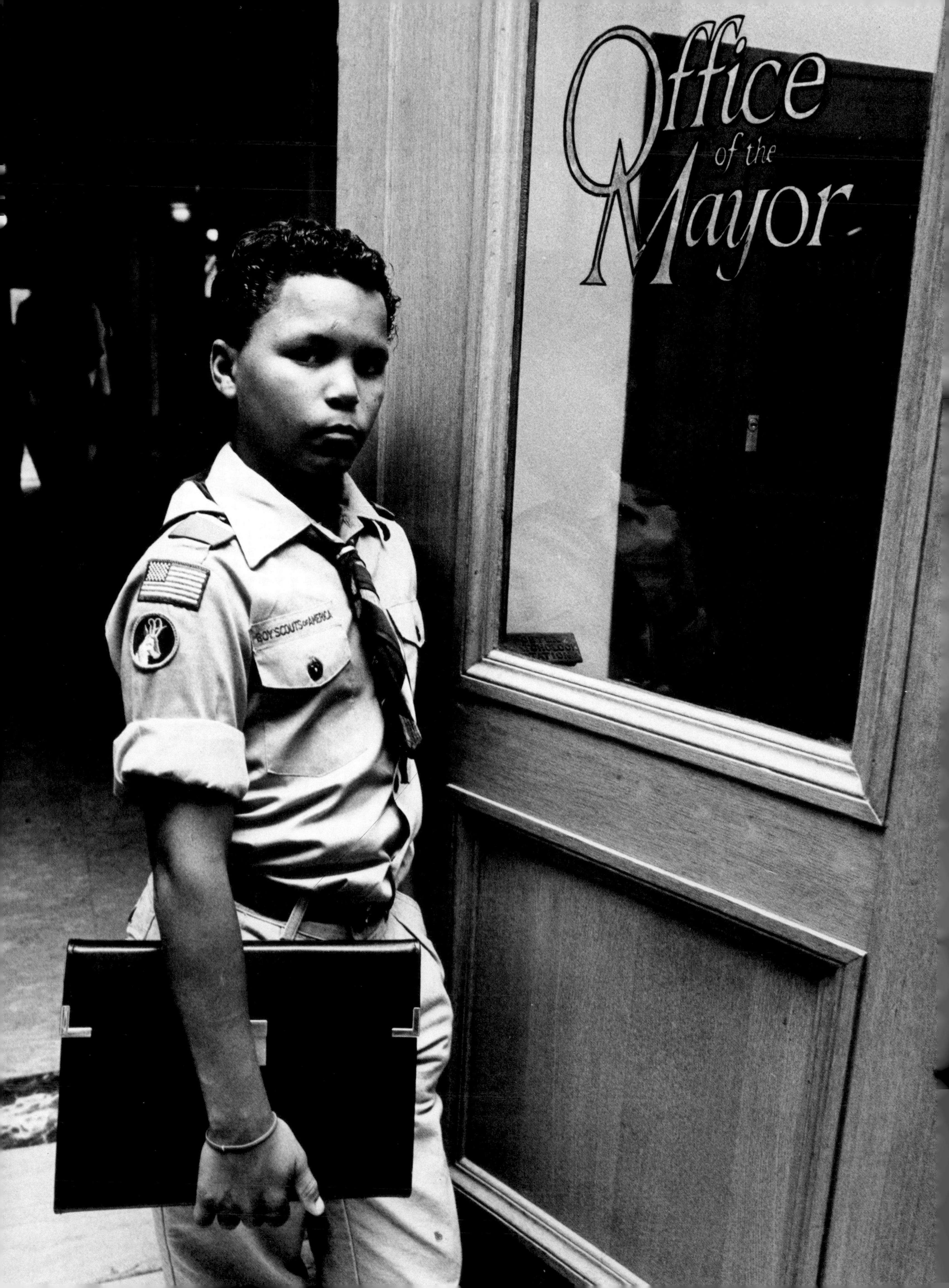
Office of the Mayor
BOY SCOUTS of AMERICA

Previous page, opposite: Segura thirteen, and his family live in a station wagon just outside of the encampment. He formed a group called Kids Helping Each Other in the campground. The original membership of fifty dwindled when a rumor circulated that children involved in the group would be taken from their parents. On August 19, 1987 Segura spoke before the Los Angeles City Council about life in the encampment. He told a Los Angeles Times reporter, "Kids like me shouldn't have to worry about feeding ourselves. We should be able to play where there isn't glass and weird people all around."
A brief, unplanned encounter with Los Angeles Mayor Bradley was disappointing. "He shook my hand and twenty seconds later he just walked away.... All I wanted to do was to tell him what it's like in the campground. I know he's a busy man but I wish he'd care a little more."

Question asked by Segura Williams of L.A.'s city council regarding life in the Urban Campground:

Questions:

1. Why won't the city, state or government help the homeless?
2. Why can't we have a better ground to live on?
3. Don't children have rights to be heard?
4. Why can't we have some medical assistance?
5. Why do we have to suffer because of politics?
6. Why does the government help people in other countries and won't help the homeless in America?
7. Why don't more people help other children?

Things we can do:

1. We can help other children around the world.
2. We can stop diseases from spreading.
3. We can talk to the school board about school buses for rides back and forth to schools.
4. We can talk to other organizations for supplying three meals a day.
5. We can help our parents get more jobs.
6. We can stop kids from getting involved in drugs.

Kids helping Each Other Temporararily from:
The Urban Campground
By Segura Williams, the President

This page:
Getting ready for school in
the urban encampment.
Los Angeles, California

Opposite:
Families do their best to
maintain a sense of
closeness and normal family
life.
Los Angeles, California

Overleaf:
Los Angeles urban
encampment.
Los Angeles, California

Previous page:
Vietnam vet at the urban
encampment.
Los Angeles, California

236

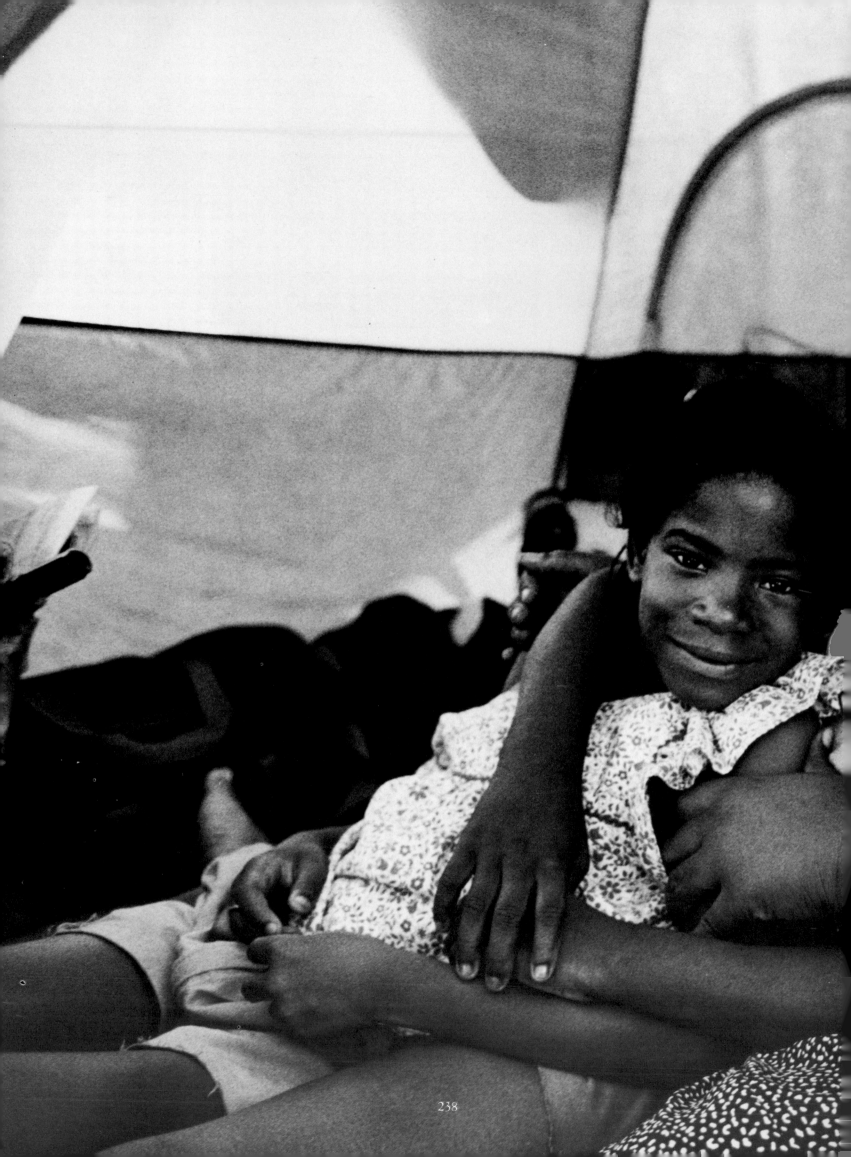

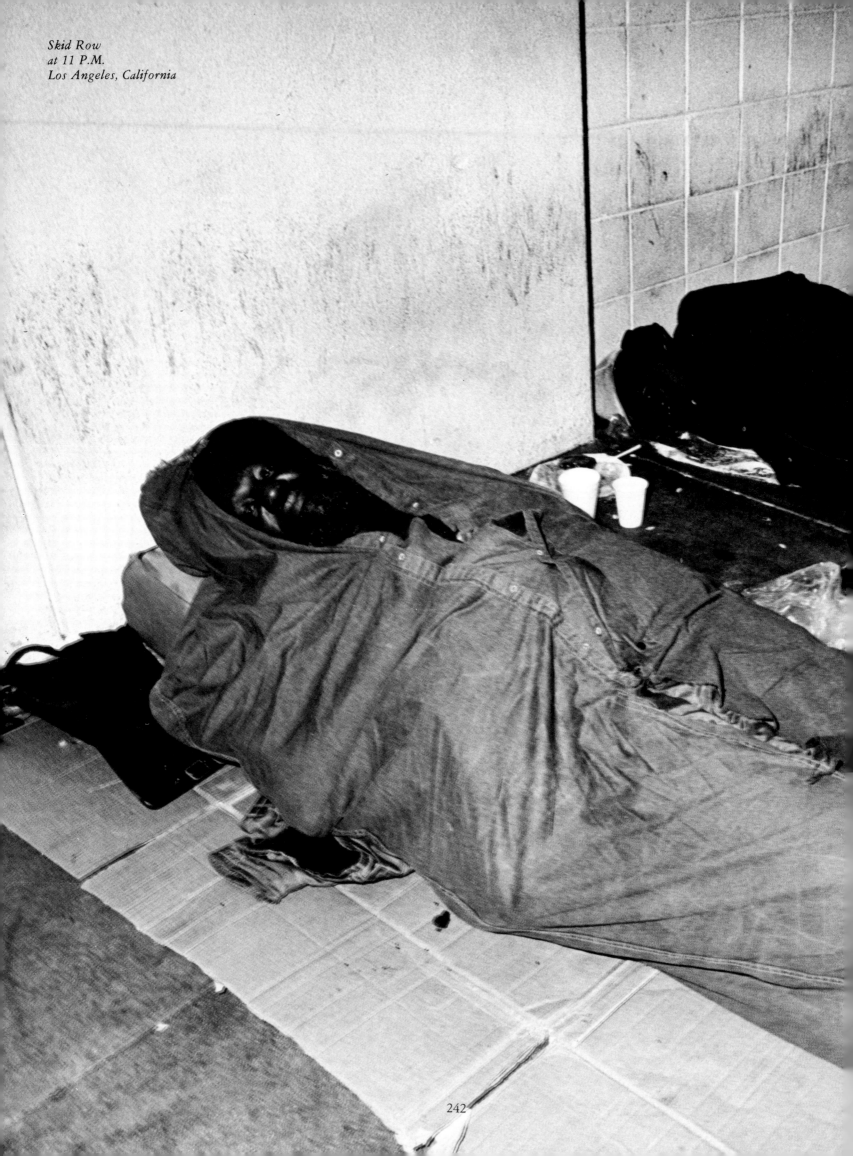

Shabbytown resident in his
improvised "home" before it
was destroyed.
Wilmington, California

Police inform Shabbytown residents that the camp is going to be demolished. Wilmington, California

This page and overleaves:
Destruction of Shabbytown.
Wilmington, California

248

We, the homeless.

AD REINHARDT

AD REINHARDT

THE MUSEUM OF CONTEMPORARY ART, LOS ANGELES

THE MUSEUM OF MODERN ART, NEW YORK

RIZZOLI, NEW YORK

PUBLISHED TO ACCOMPANY AN EXHIBITION OF THE SAME TITLE
ORGANIZED JOINTLY BY THE MUSEUM OF MODERN ART, NEW YORK,
AND THE MUSEUM OF CONTEMPORARY ART, LOS ANGELES, AND SUPPORTED BY GRANTS
FROM THE HENRY LUCE FOUNDATION, INC., AND MR. AND MRS. GILBERT H. KINNEY.

ADDITIONAL SUPPORT WAS PROVIDED BY THE NATIONAL ENDOWMENT FOR THE ARTS.

EXHIBITION SCHEDULE

THE MUSEUM OF MODERN ART, NEW YORK
MAY 30 – SEPTEMBER 2, 1991

THE MUSEUM OF CONTEMPORARY ART, LOS ANGELES
OCTOBER 13, 1991 – JANUARY 5, 1992

FIRST PUBLISHED IN THE UNITED STATES OF AMERICA IN 1991
BY RIZZOLI INTERNATIONAL PUBLICATIONS, INC.
300 PARK AVENUE SOUTH, NEW YORK, NY 10010
LIBRARY OF CONGRESS CATALOGING-IN-PUBLICATION DATA

REINHARDT, AD. 1913 – 1967.
AD REINHARDT/THE MUSEUM OF MODERN ART, NEW YORK, THE MUSEUM OF
CONTEMPORARY ART, LOS ANGELES: ESSAY BY YVE-ALAIN BOIS.
P.   CM.
INCLUDES BIBLIOGRAPHICAL REFERENCES.
ISBN 0-8478-1336-3.—ISBN 0-87070-187-8
1. REINHARDT, AD, 1913-1967—EXHIBITIONS. I. MUSEUM OF
CONTEMPORARY ART (LOS ANGELES, CALIF.) II. MUSEUM OF MODERN ART
(NEW YORK, N.Y.) III. TITLE.
ND237.R316A4   1991   759.13 — dc20   90 – 50800 CIP

DESIGNED BY STEVEN SCHOENFELDER
COMPOSITION BY GRAPHIC ARTS COMPOSITION, PHILADELPHIA
PRINTED AND BOUND BY TOPPAN PRINTING COMPANY, TOKYO, JAPAN

FRONTISPIECE: AD REINHARDT, C. 1954

CONTENTS

PREFACE   7
William Rubin

THE LIMIT OF ALMOST   11
Yve-Alain Bois

PLATES   35

CHRONOLOGY, SELECTED WRITINGS,
AND CARTOONS BY AD REINHARDT   107

EXHIBITION HISTORY   129

SELECTED BIBLIOGRAPHY   133

ACKNOWLEDGMENTS   137
Richard Koshalek and Richard E. Oldenburg

LENDERS TO THE EXHIBITION   141

AD REINHARDT, 1966.

PREFACE

The flowering of the art of painting in New York during the forties and fifties has sometimes been called an American Renaissance. And given the provincial state of the plastic arts in this country prior to World War II, that may not be hyperbole. To be sure, the period was more a birth than a rebirth as regards the native tradition. But in terms of modernist painting as a whole, which had not fared as well between the world wars as in the previous half century, and which was virtually cut off during World War II, rebirth is the right word.

As of 1966, when I came to The Museum of Modern Art, the collection was still seriously deficient in the work of the agents of this new flourishing—a pioneer generation known misleadingly as Abstract Expressionists. Therefore, over the immediately ensuing years we engaged in a campaign of acquisitions—soliciting gifts, making purchases and exchanges—with the result that the overwhelming majority of paintings and sculptures by those artists now in the Museum's collection were acquired during that time.

The net we spread was independent of any stylistic *parti pris.* Hence, although Ad Reinhardt was at odds with virtually all the aesthetic convictions and assumptions of his contemporaries, we made no less an effort to acquire his work in depth. Seven of the eight Reinhardt oils the Museum collection can show today were the fruit of that campaign. They give us an overview of his work that is unrivaled.

Not all the work of painters we collected in depth in that campaign has survived the intervening decades as well as Reinhardt's has. As I reviewed the collection galleries over the years, I became increasingly convinced by the austere splendor of his pictures, by the degree to which they compelled interest, and by their strength in relation to their neighbors. Yet, Reinhardt's peers in his generation have fared better publicly than he, some of them having received multiple museum retrospectives during recent decades, while the only American retrospective ever devoted to his work took place a quarter of a century ago, during the brief secular moment of The Jewish Museum. Moreover, that museum had but a minuscule vanguard art constituency in what was then a small art world. Out of all this came our feeling—happily shared by Richard Koshalek of The Museum of Contemporary Art, Los Angeles—that the time was more than ripe to give the public a closer look at the whole of Ad Reinhardt's career.

Ethical probity in life is not the same as ethos in painting. The ethical imperatives that give grandeur to Cézanne's work reflect not his quotidian behavior or beliefs (such as his Catholicism), but the nature of his confrontation with his art. Yet there is, I think, some sense of direct crossover in Ad Reinhardt's mature painting—an ethical stamina that recalls his uncompromisingness, his moral fervor in life. But this is perhaps the only such crossover in Reinhardt, for no other painter has ever maintained, I think, a more rigid separation of art and life. Far from painting in the "space between" them, he mounted there an almost unbreachable wall.

The extrapictorial implications of the rigor of Reinhardt's art—the puritanical aspects of which establish an astonishing tension between their own austerity and the glowing sensuousness they nevertheless make possible—strike me as a not inapt message for the art world that has evolved since his death. Nonfigurative as well as Pop-related painting has increasingly privileged those styles that favor instantaneous delivery and maximal immediate impact over the solicitation of searching, meditative viewing. The visitor who "does" the Ad Reinhardt retrospective at three miles an hour will literally not see it, for the purely optical adjustment that Reinhardt's later paintings posit as a prerequisite to the real experience of the picture constitutes a kind of willed barrier. This requirement testifies to the dislike, indeed fear, of being too readily understood, which Reinhardt shared with his generation. There is, of course, nothing inherently good or bad about "difficult" art as compared to that which aims for instantaneous comprehension. But there is a great difference in the character of the experience they communicate. For all his differences with his coevals, Reinhardt shows himself in this regard as more a member of the Abstract Expressionist generation than that of the Minimalists who were subsequently drawn to his art.

Reinhardt's later work obviously constitutes an extreme of the taste for reductiveness that forms a leitmotif in twentieth-century art. But for such members of his own generation as Barnett Newman and Mark Rothko, aesthetic reductiveness was in no way meant to imply or connote a delimitation of the range or variety of experience. (Hence, Rothko's insistence that his painting was "more violent" than Pollock's.) However, Reinhardt's pursuit of a maximally spare, static, iconic image he would call "timeless"—an image that wedded his passion for Western classicism and Eastern monism—involved a determined narrowing of the pictorial experience. To be sure, Reinhardt expressed his full share of anger and violence as well as playfulness, wit, and love of give-and-take. But not in his art. These and many other areas of the human drama are evidenced only in his life—and, more particularly, in his pronouncements,

cartoons, and missives, which together clearly acted as a kind of socially purposeful safety valve necessary to the pursuit of his exclusive artistic ideal.

We judge art, however, not by what the artist doesn't do but by what he does. And if the range of experience in Reinhardt's painting increasingly narrowed, the quality of his work became increasingly profound. He seemed instinctively compelled to reduce the picture to that area in which he could make his most individual, most personal statement. All the definitions and rules he promulgated came afterward, as rationalizations. The drama of Reinhardt's career is in this focusing down, which required not only an intense concentration, but an almost manic will. Characteristics of his early and middle periods, such as lyricism and luminosity, were not rejected but distilled—and distilled again. We feel that the faint light which emanates from the resplendent "black" pictures that end his career is the vestige of the refiner's fire.

William Rubin
Director Emeritus
Department of Painting and Sculpture
The Museum of Modern Art

A ''BLACK'' PAINTING BEING EXECUTED BY AD REINHARDT, 1966.

THE LIMIT OF ALMOST

YVE-ALAIN BOIS

"The first paintings which cannot be misunderstood," wrote Ad Reinhardt, perhaps as a description of his "black" paintings, but more likely as a programmatic invocation related to them.[1] He also could have written: "the first paintings which cannot be understood," or rather, "which *should* not be understood." In other words, there is nothing there to be "understood" (to be explained, interpreted, deciphered). What is at issue, indeed, as Reinhardt jotted down just a few lines below in the same passage, is a "sign which refuses to signify."[2] Of course he knew, maybe better than anyone else, that this was ontologically impossible: signs signify, which is why they are called signs, and "a sign refusing to signify" in fact signifies this very refusal—that is, quite a lot. Of all the artists with whom he is usually associated, all of them so vocal about subject matter, Reinhardt had the most refined conception of meaning, a differential conception actually very close to that elaborated in structuralist analyses of language and myth. His "what is not there is more important than what is there"[3] is a direct echo, involuntary or not, of Ferdinand de Saussure's "in language there are only differences" and of Claude Lévi-Strauss's "a myth signifies primarily by what it chooses to exclude."[4] Or, to put it another way, the more one refuses, the more one signifies, and therefore, conversely, "the more stuff that's in a painting, the simpler it is."[5] "Less is more," but "more is less."[6] Hence Reinhardt's numerous negative statements; hence what I would call his oxymoronic and asymptotic logic, always almost an illogic—in the same way that his late canvases are always almost black. ("Black" should be thought of between quotation marks when applied to Reinhardt's canvases dating from 1954 to the end of his life in 1967, the inverted comma being one of Reinhardt's favorite modes of ironical distancing in his writings.) I will return to this almostness, which is the core of the matter.

Reinhardt knew that signs never fail to signify, that works never fail to be "understood" (explained, interpreted, deci-phered), which is to say misunderstood in the usual sense of the word. Yet he strove to create "the first paintings which cannot be misunderstood." Such an endeavor entails immense risks and impediments (to prevent "understanding" from sneaking in, to cut short the compulsion to interpret seems necessarily quixotic). It also presupposes a tremendous faith. Reinhardt liked to draft lists of labels he had been allotted, in order (usually) to disallow them: "negativist" is one of them (along with "classicist," "purist," "avant-gardist," "Orientalist," "religious painter," "ivory towerist," and many others).[7] For once, I think, such denials ought to be taken in earnest: his negations are affirmative statements, as when he stresses "the intellectual power of *asserting* 'not.'"[8] Reinhardt for me is the least pessimistic artist, his art the most expectant. Confronted with what he saw and denounced in his moralistic, witty satires and cartoons, as the growing power of the forces of "darkness" (corruption of the art world, debasement of art into entertainment, and so on), he patiently pursued his work "as if those who are going to read us [to look at our art, we might add] will belong to a civilization more delicate and subtle than any we know."[9] How could it be otherwise? How could someone stick to his guns as much as Reinhardt did and not convey, if it did not sound a bit too pollyannaish, what we would call a message of hope. There is a prophetic tone in Reinhardt's art and discourse, for part of him is akin to Moses (that other great iconoclast): one cannot claim for oneself the title of "the first post-historic artist" without having envisioned something like a Promised Land.

Yet Reinhardt's works *were* and have been misunderstood, more vastly perhaps than the art of anyone else—certainly more than that of any of his contemporaries. They either have left critics at bay (perhaps a lesser evil), or they have led, constantly, inevitably, to various misinterpretations. Not that no one has been able, so far, to engage with the irreducible difficulty of his art and to provide accurate guidelines for its apprehension. But it seems to me that misreadings have by far dominated Reinhardt's criticism, the most vociferous and damaging of all being well-disposed, consisting of sympathetic reappropriations by artists and critics of a younger generation.

Why is that? In her pioneering book on Reinhardt, Lucy Lippard states that "he was a 'thirties painter' in the forties and a 'sixties painter' in the fifties."[10] There is a great deal of truth to this, but I would qualify the second half of the statement: in a way, I am not sure that Reinhardt ever was a painter of the sixties although the late recognition he enjoyed, in the sixties precisely, was due to the fact that he was thought so, as if he had finally decided or managed to be his own contemporary. The story, which can be summarized in three acts, is well known. (The first two acts border on the scandalous and account for the growing amount of bitterness or resentment to be found in Reinhardt's relationship with the art establishment toward the end of his life.)

Act One. At the end of 1959, Reinhardt asked the Whitney Museum of American Art to offer him a retrospective of twenty-five years of his work, a request that was refused. He subsequently organized it himself the following year at Betty Parsons's satellite gallery, Section Eleven,[11] while presenting at the gallery proper, not coincidentally, his first "Ultimate Paintings," freshly painted (1960), along with other, previous "black" canvases of 1954–59 (from then on, Reinhardt would only paint "black," square canvases, five feet by five feet). The exhibition had been "closely paralleled by Martin James's excellent article," noted Lawrence Campbell in Art News, referring to the first serious attempt to deal with Reinhardt's career as a whole.[12] Given the meticulous staging, timing, and care that surrounded the preparation of this double show, the reviews must have been an immense disappointment to Reinhardt.

Act Two. After another one-man show, at the Dwan Gallery in Los Angeles, and his participation, always willy-nilly, in several miscellaneous group exhibitions, Reinhardt was at last invited to send some of his recent work to one of The Museum of Modern Art's "selection" shows ("Americans 1963"). In 1963 the Modern had finally bought a "black" canvas: even if belatedly, the institution was standing by him.[13] Once again, however, Reinhardt was right to feel ill-presented to the public, for this show, like the preceding ones of its kind, was definitely a mixed bag: what did he, the dean of American abstract art (he was proud of being unique, in this country, for having started as an abstract painter), have to do with "young talents" such as Claes Oldenburg, Robert Indiana, Lee Bontecou, Chryssa, Marisol, James Rosenquist, and other (since forgotten) object-makers, most of them born twenty years after he was?[14] Furthermore, the canvases were badly installed (much too brightly lit, roped off, and hung too high so that people would keep their hands off them). The fact that the few favorable reviewers noted this last misfortune (which would recur time and again, to Reinhardt's dismay), but not the incongruity of his company, is telling: Reinhardt was beginning to be seen as an "artist of the sixties," as an heir of Marcel Duchamp.

Act Three. Frustrated by the outcome of these events, Reinhardt decided to strike a great and definitive blow. In 1965 he organized a three-gallery exhibition (one gallery for his blue canvases of 1950–53, one for his red canvases of the same period, one for his "black" paintings of 1954–65). The reviewers once again displayed their total puzzlement (and Reinhardt's participation, earlier the same year, in the famous "Responsive Eye" exhibition at the Modern did not help much, providing ground for one of the most common misreadings, that of his work as a forerunner of Op art). Yet things had begun to change. The general press continued to bark or laugh, but Reinhardt's 1963 appearance had produced its effect among a whole group of artists (and a lesser group of critics), as if his radical foreignness in the landscape of "Americans 1963" had at last managed to catch the eyes of the spectators, while his showing in contexts seemingly more appropriate to his art, with artists seemingly closer to him, had gone entirely unnoticed. This effect was now consolidating. My contention, however, is that the sudden availability of Reinhardt, biased as it was by the hyped debates of the time, was misfiring—that it was the result of an anachronistic illusion. Apart from Priscilla Colt's sensible article in Art International in 1964, which warned against looking at Reinhardt's canvases as if they were pure monochromes (hence objects) and had given the best account, thus far, of the phenomenological transformation his art implies, the interpretation offered in the few intelligent commentaries of the mid-sixties was that of Reinhardt as the father of Minimalism (see Barbara Rose's influential "ABC Art," for example, which appeared roughly at the time of the triple exhibition).[15] Reinhardt had found an audience: the final consecration, which came a year later with his "retrospective" at The Jewish Museum, was the direct result of this new, but deceptive, accessibility.[16] This came in extremis: the Jewish Museum show opened on November 23, 1966, and closed on January 15, 1967; Reinhardt died on August 31, 1967.

Two years later, Reinhardt's ultimate (and posthumous) association with the art of the sixties, based more on his theoretical work than on his paintings, was his canonization as the guru of yet another movement, Conceptual art. Despite a few solitary voices going against the consensus (notably Dore Ashton in a perceptive review of the Jewish Museum show), despite a few later amends (that of Barbara Rose, for example), and despite Lucy Lippard's 1966 catalogue and her more recent monograph (with its glaring evidence that the case has been ill-defined from the start and closed too swiftly), the labels "Minimalist" or "Conceptualist" have adhered to Reinhardt to this day as much as that of "mystic," and have prevented a genuine understanding of his art (that is, as we have seen, its non-understanding).[17]

Yet if any reading is a misreading, any misreading is a reading (which is somewhat better, it seems, than no reading at all). The Minimalist or Conceptualist interpretations of Reinhardt *were* productive, for they at last provided his art with a framework through which it could be seen, and his texts could be read. These interpretations were also not entirely wrong. After all, Reinhardt's canvases—which, as he among others noted, did "not hang easily in group shows"[18] since everything alongside them had a tendency to appear fussy—felt remarkably at home in the company of works by Carl Andre, Jo Baer, Dan Flavin, Donald Judd, Sol LeWitt, Agnes Martin, Robert Morris, Michael Steiner, and Robert Smithson at the exhibition entitled "10" held at the Dwan Gallery (1966–67), perhaps the strongest Minimalist definitional statement ever made. (Again, despite Reinhardt's multiple statements against sculpture in general, nobody seemed to notice at the time the bizarreness of this association of his art with sculptural practitioners.)[19] In the same manner, Reinhardt's "art-as-art" dogma and his incantatory negations could be easily rescued from "meaninglessness" by the nominalist stance of the theoreticians of Conceptual art (notwithstanding the fact that such a rescue was the last thing he would have called for).[20] Yet the affinities are purely morphological: Joseph Kosuth's "art-as-idea-as-idea" only *looks* (a bit) like "art-as-art," and nothing is more foreign to Reinhardt than what Michael Fried defined as the theatrical conditions of Minimal art ("Theater, acting, 'lowest of the arts,'" wrote Reinhardt).[21] Many other signs point to what separates Reinhardt's aesthetic from that of Minimal or Conceptual artists. For example, he was vehemently against the paterfamilias of both movements ("I've never approved or liked anything about Marcel Duchamp. You have to choose between Duchamp and Mondrian"),[22] and in-

deed he found the whole Duchampian slogan of filling the gap "between art and life" as repulsive as the hybridization between the individual arts. Furthermore, he insisted, especially at the end of his life, on the fact that there were "no good ideas in art;"[23] and finally, responding specifically to the Minimalist credo, he refused to consider phenomenal, literal space as one of the perceptual parameters of art (his abhorrence of the gloss on a painting's surface, which led to his drastically grayed-out canvases, which in turn accounts for their extreme fragility, had much to do with his fear of interference of actual space caused by reflections).

Numerous other evidences could be cited to show that Reinhardt is neither a Minimal nor a Conceptual artist (I am temporarily holding in abeyance the issue of the mystical interpretation), but I will rest my case. Yet one might still wonder why I have devoted so much space to defining what he is *not* rather than what he *is*. In doing so, I am deliberately following Reinhardt's instructions: "The only way to say what an artist-as-artist is is to say what an artist-as-artist is not";[24] "the one struggle in art is the struggle of artists against artists";[25] and, finally, and more important, "you can only make absolute statements negatively."[26] The only way to say what Reinhardt's art is (that is, to make an absolute statement), is to say what it is not. Although my strategy (borrowing Reinhardt's own) might seem a bit coy, it is the only one possible—it is entirely programmed by the exigencies of Reinhardt's art itself.

First, this strategy (Reinhardt's) relies on a strategic conception of art and of history. Reinhardt's tongue-in-cheek longing for an Academy must be read in this light, for academies, historically speaking—in Florence during the Renaissance, in seventeenth-century Paris—have been polemical enterprises of separation, of war, as he himself noted: war against the guilds and against the confusion of art with craft. Every "revolution in art," says Reinhardt, has yielded a redefinition of art, and each revolution has involved a secession: "In the eighteenth century, 'aesthetics' was invented to isolate art from other fields. In the nineteenth century, the main art movements were all involved with 'independence'—independence from something. In the twentieth century, the central question in art was the 'purity' of art." Hence, abstraction: "the word 'abstract' was a new attempt to separate and define art."[27] Similarly, "the still life, landscape, the pure still life and the pure landscape and the pure portrait were negations of all kinds of narrative, mythological, and historical painting."[28] Anyone interested in the development of recent

13

historiography cannot help but notice the similarity of Reinhardt's brilliant conception of history with that of structuralism[29]; any avid reader of his writings (and I hold them among the most cogent texts written by an artist during this loquacious century, certainly the most pointed) cannot fail to see how this strategy informs his aesthetic.

Furthermore, this strategic conception of art and history dispenses with historicism, that plight of modernism: a strategic field is necessarily closed. If history has to be thought of as evolution at all, it can only take the shape of a spiral; there can be no end nor can there be any beginning: "the end is always a beginning."[30] The whole notion of the "death" of art (or of painting) is ridiculous, not only because art is always already "dead"[31] (it is not an organism), but because this death would presuppose a horizon beyond the field, which is both naive and impossible. Reinhardt was remarkably consistent about this at the end of his career. One of his last statements reads: "If I were to say that I am making the last paintings, I don't mean that painting is dying. You go back to the beginning all the time anyway."[32] Hence (and he makes the connection himself), his tongue-in-cheek titles: *Ultimate Painting No. 39*, *Timeless Painting, 1960*. Hence, also, his constant invocation of a "tradition" of the "last painting": "I often feel I'm inventing a new language, the language of Manet, Monet, Mondrian, Malevich."[33] If "painting" is to be defined strategically, as a game (like chess, for example, that master-game of strategy), and modern art as a particular match or series of matches of that game, then the issue of the end of painting becomes irrelevant (a game, generically speaking, does not end), and that of the end of modern art becomes immediately that of its beginning (every chess player knows that the end of a match is, by itself, the beginning of another one). No wonder, then, that Reinhardt felt so attracted to the historian George Kubler's *The Shape of Time* (1962), which he reviewed enthusiastically: Kubler's idea that the field of art was closed, that the possibilities of art were finite, far from yielding to an apocalyptic doom, represented for Reinhardt the most powerful confirmation of his own theory.

The field is closed, circumscribed, and it is the field of endless battles. To Reinhardt, "The first word to be spoken by [the] artist must be [a] word spoken against artists."[34] Art must affirm itself negatively; every artist must be at war, especially with those whose art seems to evolve in the same direction as one's own. This might explain how (along with Joyce, Mallarmé, Flaubert, and Melville) Reinhardt could deem Thomas Mann, hardly a companion to those "masters of voidness" (Reinhardt's expression), a writer after his own heart—Mann, who recalls his displeasure at reading his old friend Hermann Hesse's *Magister Ludi* and finding it much too similar to his own work ("to be reminded that one is not alone in the world—always unpleasant," he wrote in his diary, adding this quotation from Goethe: "Do we then live if others live?").[35]

But the issue is far more important than a search for originality. In fact, it is the other way around. Reinhardt's originality lies in the oxymoronic use he makes of the strategic model, perhaps the most complex and important point of his aesthetic: his strategy is aimed against art-as-strategy, art-as-play, art-as-agon. His chess playing is entirely directed against painting-as-chess playing, against painting-as-struggle or drama, against the against.[36] In other words, it is directed against the art of everyone else—almost—which is both the only logical position and the most difficult one: "I heard someone say that it is easy to attack everything, and I have been thinking about how difficult it is. I would like to attack almost everything."[37]

Another detour will supply an entry into the heart of the matter, that is, the magnificent paradox of Reinhardt's art, its agonistic struggle against agon. As pointed out, Reinhardt was vastly misunderstood. He knew that this was inevitable: "To endure (not to be understood)."[38] But even if the fervor of most of his supporters amounted to Judas kisses, it did give him, as also pointed out earlier, a belated "visibility." But how? What obstacle could have been suddenly removed, in the mid-sixties, so that this "visibility," no matter how deceptive, could have become at all possible? Joseph Kosuth provided, if unwittingly, the beginning of an answer when he asked, in 1969: "How . . . can one account for, given [Clement Greenberg's] theories—if they have any logic to them at all—his disinterest in Frank Stella, Ad Reinhardt, and others applicable to his historical scheme?"[39] Kosuth's reply to this question—that Clement Greenberg's indifference to both painters of "black" canvases was only a matter of his personal distaste—is by no means erroneous: in fact, by introducing the issue of a contradiction between Greenberg's theories and his taste, Kosuth says much more than he himself realizes. But it is insufficient, for indeed it was the polarization of American art discourse with regard to Greenberg's modernist formalism around 1961–62 (with the publication of "Modernist Painting" and "After Abstract Expressionism")[40] that created a climate in which Reinhardt's art became suddenly noticeable. An oppositional paradigm was formed: one was either for or against; one was either in or out of Greenberg's canon, and if one was out, one paid renewed attention to one's outcast colleagues.

The logic and necessity of Greenberg's rejection of (or silence on) Frank Stella's black paintings has been brilliantly demonstrated by Thierry de Duve, for whom "After Abstract Expressionism" is a key text, and rightly so.[41] In it Greenberg posits explicitly but paradoxically, playing the devil's advocate, what had been implicit for two decades as the essential horizon of painting, its limit or zero degree ("a stretched or tacked up canvas already exists as a picture—though not necessarily a *successful* one").[42] It was precisely because Stella's black paintings looked *almost* like this, ready-made, because it seemed that they had provided a stupefying materialization of his theory, so to speak, that Greenberg had to reverse gears and to consolidate his fiction of a "pure opticality" into a clear demarcation between pictoriality and objecthood.

But the danger represented by Stella's 1959 paintings for Greenberg's modernist stance had already been defused, premonitorily as it were, by his writings in 1958 (thus immediately preceding the paintings' explosive arrival), including the rewriting of various texts for their later inclusion in *Art and Culture* (most dramatically, "The New Sculpture" of 1948, the famous essay on Cubist papier collé, and, most important, a defense of Hans Hofmann). Reinhardt might have played the role of catalyst in Greenberg's sudden urge to amend himself in 1958, but this role should not be exaggerated (Greenberg's position on many issues had started to shift five years earlier with his discovery of Morris Louis). It is true that the famous "Twelve Rules for a New Academy" appeared in *Art News* in 1957, and at that time they *could* (but in retrospect ought not to) be read as a caricature of Greenberg's vision of modernism as an enterprise of reduction, self-purification, and auto-definition. But, from Greenberg's point of view, there was more urgent business to attend to: Jasper Johns's art (which made the cover of *Art News* in January 1958) was also dangerously close to what Greenberg had been theoretically advocating, and an article by Allan Kaprow, fueling the gruesome myth of action painting by attributing to Jackson Pollock the paternity of his Happenings, was published in *Art News* right between Greenberg's essays on Cubist collage and on Hofmann.[43]

Greenberg was uninterested in Stella's black paintings for many of the same reasons he actively opposed the work of Reinhardt (which we shall see presently), but as far as Stella is concerned, they are not as important. The main issue in his disapproving silence in front of Stella's works, as de Duve has shown so well, concerned the dismantling, or at least radical questioning, of the opposition between the "specificity of painting" and the "genericity of art"—which is the problem raised by Duchamp. As Greenberg was perfectly aware, this problem has nothing to do with Reinhardt.[44] But Greenberg's rewriting, the reshuffling of his theory (which in some cases seems to be almost an about-face), the sudden pulling out of his trump card, Hofmann—all this has much to do with Reinhardt.

The issues are quite complex. To summarize the argument at the outset: it was only around 1957–58 that Greenberg realized that he had been a "Hofmannian" all along, but not a consistent enough one. The name of his Viennese-born teacher is indeed invoked in Greenberg's writings right from the start (1939).[45] But those early invocations are always qualified. In a review of the painter's second one-man show, in 1945, Greenberg stresses his debt to Hofmann's theories but is critical of his paintings.[46] In "The Present Prospect of American Painting and Sculpture," which appeared two years later, while again praising Hofmann's teaching, Greenberg states that his "spiritual" terminology is counter-intuitive (it "may mislead at first") and—against all evidence—writes that "Hofmann's approach, in spite of himself and his own verbalizations, is essentially a positivist one."[47] It is only in 1957–58 that Greenberg's claims for Hofmann become extravagant, notably in a retrospective article about the thirties written as an exhibition review. (This was published, incidentally, in the issue of *Art News* following that in which the "Twelve Rules" appeared, and it contains a critical remark about Reinhardt that would be dropped in the *Art and Culture* version of the piece: "Reinhardt's collage of 1940 anticipates the kind of brittle late Cubism done in Paris after 1945, and says much for the sophistication of American painting in 1940, but it is the end of something, not the beginning.")[48] Here Hofmann and his school figure at last as the major pole of this historical period, the thirties (the other being the American Abstract Artists group, the A.A.A., as a whole "from which some abstract painters learned at least what they did *not* want to do"); through Hofmann, it is said, "you could learn more about Matisse's color than from Matisse himself."[49] A year and a half later, the same argument would be directed toward Cubism: "No one has digested Cubism more thoroughly than Hofmann, and perhaps no one has better conveyed its gist to others"[50] (even if it was to note that his alleged debt to Cubism had been more a handicap than anything else).

Indeed, Cubism is at stake; not Cubism per se but the interpretation of Cubism as a critical stance. With remarkable honesty, in "After Abstract Expressionism" Greenberg himself points to this issue as central (the essay is to be read, then, both as a retrospective analysis of his progressive *aggiornamento*, which began in the early fifties, and as the definitive constitution of the dogma). Greenberg refers to an attack against his art criticism, which appeared in 1948 in *Partisan Review*, written by George L. K. Morris, the brilliant spokesman of the A.A.A. (and a close friend of Reinhardt): "he took me to task for, among other things, preferring what he called 'behind the frame' painting. . . . His dogmatism did not take away from the acuteness of his 'behind-the-frame' characterization, especially in its implications, *as I only later came to recognize*. Hofmann's and Pollock's and Gorky's pictures did stay further behind their frames than Mondrian's or than Picasso's post-1913 pictures did."[51]

The extraordinary structure of the chess match we are witnessing here is that of a *chassé-croisé* with Cubism as the main stake. This round (in three moves) starts with two articles by Greenberg that prompt Morris's criticism: "The Present Prospect . . . ," mentioned earlier (in which the A.A.A. was totally ignored), published in October 1947; and "The Decline of Cubism," which appeared in March 1948. First move: In the latter essay Greenberg defines Cubism as a sort of optimistic "positivism," insisting on its anti-illusionist flatness and its assertion of the medium of painting, and explains its ebbing, in the thirties, by a waning of "the empiricist's faith in the supreme reality of concrete experience" that had characterized it earlier (one example given by Greenberg of this decline must have been particularly irritating to Morris, that of the alleged "weakening Mondrian's art suffered between 1937 and his death in 1944").[52]

Second move: in June 1948, Morris replies that Greenberg is totally off the mark, that the Cubists were never positivist anti-illusionists (for one thing, their works were always figurative). "The 'window-conception' remains, even if it is a window with the shutters closed." By contrast, a "contemporary abstract painting" (that is, the product of the A.A.A.), being flat and non-representational, advocates its internal structure: "instead of being a window bordered by a frame, [it] becomes an object itself." Morris concludes his diatribe by noting that "the worst that an Abstractionist can say of one of his fellows is that he is 'stuck in Cubism,'" a reproach, significantly, that Greenberg himself will later use against Hofmann to disparage his unsuccessful canvases.[53]

Third move: Greenberg takes his turn (his response is published together with Morris's essay). True, the Cubist canvas was ambiguous during the Analytic phase, "leaving the eye to doubt whether the image or rather the pictorial complex came forward or receded. But . . . its inherent, irrevocable (and historical) tendency was to drive the picture plane forward so that it became identical with the physical surface of the canvas itself. This tendency makes itself very evident in Picasso's and Braque's first collages." In other words, "It belongs to the importance of Cubism . . . that it conclusively liquidated the illusion of the third dimension. It did not have to wait for Malevich or Mondrian to do that."[54] In a review, published a few months later, of "Collage," a Museum of Modern Art exhibition, Greenberg's position on Cubist papier collé is even starker: with the collage, the surface of the work of art became completely opaque, not only eliminating the *illusion* of the third dimension (making "the picture indissolubly one with the pigment, the texture, and the flat surface that constituted it as an object"), but advocating a passage to *real* three-dimensionality, a passage of the picture into the realm of things. "Painting was being transformed, in the course of a strictly coherent process with a logic of its own, into a new kind of sculpture"—the same logic that much later led Stella's black paintings to look almost like objects.[55]

To anyone familiar with Greenberg's extraordinary collage essay of 1958 ("The Pasted Paper Revolution," later simply entitled "Collage" in *Art and Culture*), it is apparent that it reversed *all* the assertions of the 1948 piece. The reason is simple: in 1948, when Greenberg referred to Cubism, he meant Synthetic Cubism, for its characteristics—assertive flatness, tactility, and the like—were the theoretical tools he thought most appropriate for describing the art he wanted to defend. (Thus, for example, he wrote in "The Present Prospects . . .": "Pollock's strength lies in the emphatic surfaces of his pictures, which it is his concern to maintain and intensify in all that thick, fuliginous flatness which began— but only began—to be the strong point of late cubism.")[56] By 1958, the master trope had become Analytic Cubism (residual illusion, opticality, and so on), for none of the terms Greenberg had previously identified with Cubism (that is, in fact, with Synthetic Cubism) would fit Morris Louis's interpretation of late Pollock (which Greenberg saw as one of the only possible avenues for the future of painting). The most important endeavor, then, was to discard as purely fictional the flatness and objecthood of Synthetic Cubism previously so strongly advocated, and to reread the entire evolution of Cubism through the lens of Analytic Cubism. Conversely, Pollock's "classic" period (1947–50) gradually ceased to be associated with Synthetic Cubism in Greenberg's criticism (from 1955 on, in fact), to become essentially dependent on Analytic Cubism's "shallow depth."[57]

Yet, there is an element of Analytic Cubism that Greenberg was willing to call upon in 1948: the tendency toward the "all-over." As Greenberg was quick to gather from the negative comments of the time, the all-over was the major symptom of a "crisis of the easel picture." But the important essay from April 1948 that bears this title should not be read as the positive manifesto it has often been taken to be: on the contrary, everything tends to indicate that Greenberg was ill at ease with the issue. For one thing, as François-Marc Gagnon has scrupulously established, *all* Greenberg's reviews of Pollock's exhibitions up to that point severely criticize the paintings that lack compositional centering and variety, and praise those that transcend the "danger of monotony."[58] The theme of the mural as Pollock's pictorial horizon, however, had already appeared in a 1947 review but only as a puzzled question mark.[59] In the "Crisis" essay, it is subsumed in a critical opposition that would come handily to release Greenberg from his doubts: there are two kinds of painting, easel painting, with its figure/ground contrast and its compositional dynamism (no matter how flat it looks), and the all-over canvas (non-hierarchical, uniform), which seems to be almost decorative, almost wallpaper, almost a mural, and which will eventually supersede the old form. These cannot be judged by the same critical tools, yet Greenberg proceeds to do exactly that. First, he perceptively disclaims for Mondrian's Neoplastic works the quality of all-overness (his pictures "constitute the flattest of all easel painting, but strong, dominating forms, as provided by intersecting straight lines and blocks of color, are still insisted upon, and the canvas, as simplified and balanced as it is, still presents itself as the *scene* of forms rather than as one single, indivisible piece of texture").[60] Further on in the essay, however, when he offers a definition of the all-over, it is Mondrian's concept of *equivalence*, including its social overtones, that he calls upon (in which, it should be remembered, one thing is always cancelled out by its opposite). The unity, the de-hierarchization of Mondrian's paintings, was hard-won, as Greenberg

had himself noted previously; it was the result of an agonistic struggle. In understanding the uniformity of the all-over painting as the product of a similar process (and Greenberg's aesthetic is agonistic through and through), he was now reinstating the traditional values associated with the notion of composition at the exact juncture at which a threat of their annihilation was perceptible. Greenberg's "crisis," at any rate, is a very short affair: all his subsequent commentaries on Pollock's works would insist on the fact that "they belong very much to the easel painting," as he writes of *Number One* (1948) in February 1949.[61]

Why does all this matter? Why all this fuss about Cubism and the all-over? In what way could this affect an investigation of Reinhardt's art? I believe that Reinhardt was perhaps the only American artist in the forties (that is, after his student work in post–Synthetic Cubism) to understand what the real issues were at the time. In this sense, but only in this sense—because he perceived things that became clear only much later—he was already (even before the fifties) an artist of the sixties. But Lucy Lippard's other assertion, that he was "an artist of the thirties" during the forties, is at least equally correct in that he decided at that time to attend to what seemed to be unfinished business. Reinhardt was the only one, at any rate, to understand that the forties debate was ill-defined: that Morris, his mentor, was right in asserting even Synthetic Cubism's failure to dispense with illusion, but wrong in assuming that abstract art had finally won the battle; that Greenberg was right in assuming that abstract art, particularly the geometric abstract art of the American Abstract Artists, a blending of, for example, Gleizes and Hélion (see fig. 1), had become an academicism, and that Mondrian's paintings in particular had never fulfilled the program of absolute flatness, despite the painter's credo; but that Greenberg was completely wrong in linking the homogeneous surface of the all-over canvas with the compositional balance inherited from Synthetic Cubism, with the notion of a dialectical "push and pull," in order to retrieve repetitiousness from the danger of a "hallucinated uniformity." Reinhardt understood that Morris and Greenberg were unaware of a common ground at the basis of their pronouncements, that of an aesthetic of the hard-won rooted in Mondrian, of the final victory of formal unity over the devil heterogeneity—Hegel's dream, if you wish. It is at this point that the Hofmann model intersects with a direct confrontation with Reinhardt's art.

FIG. 1. JEAN HÉLION. *COMPOSITION.* APRIL–MAY 1934. OIL ON CANVAS, 56¾ × 78¾" (144.3 × 199.8 CM). THE SOLOMON R. GUGGENHEIM MUSEUM, NEW YORK

The issue, which has to do with the radical incompatibility of Reinhardt's system with Greenberg's, and a fortiori, with the general aesthetic expectations in America until the sixties, can be introduced by Greenberg's judgment of 1967: "Reinhardt has a genuine if small gift for color, but none at all for design or placing." This, of course, is what all Hofmann's art, his "push and pull," is about.[62] That such a thing as a gift for design or placing should be considered a necessity for the realization of any painting is precisely what Reinhardt's entire enterprise from 1940 on was made to fight. One could even say that his art stated (among other things) that, for a painting to fail, it had only to make use of such a gift. The demonstration, if one could characterize the career of a painter that way, was long and meandering, but its outcome utterly successful: one of the things Reinhardt's "black" paintings achieved, for a whole generation of artists, was to render Hofmann's art, for example, absolutely unbearable and (to use Greenberg's rhetoric), to "clear the way . . . for things to come."[63]

Reinhardt did not deal with Hofmann per se, his teaching, or the push and the pull (he just made fun of it, but no more than of everyone else—certainly no more than of the rhetoric of de Kooning or Motherwell). He had much bigger fish to fry and no need to tackle the issue by dealing with the belated epiphenomenon of Hofmann (and I will follow his direction). As Margit Rowell has perceptively noted, the real obstacle, the real challenge, was Mondrian (there was no way to make his canvases look hideous or even unnecessary: the paintings of the Dutch master are at least as demanding as those of Reinhardt; they, too, "do not hang well in group shows").[64] In his reexamination of Mondrian's art (that is, of the *relational* aesthetic of painting, the "you-do-something-in-one-corner-and-you-balance-it-with-something-in-the-other-corner" thing, as Stella put it), in his critique of the basis of the thirties aesthetic, Reinhardt's approach was head-on.

In 1940, after a few years of the late-Cubist compositions that typified the American Abstract Artists, Reinhardt launched what amounted to a sort of time bomb (one that took a while to explode, but the sheer threat of which produced immediate effects in his own work): a perfectly modular grid painting, the first, to my knowledge, on this side of the Atlantic (*Abstract Painting*, plate, p. 38, left).[65] Grids have been recognized as the emblem of modernist painting, and correctly so,[66] but when it comes to actual modular grids, the number of occurrences is singularly small prior to Reinhardt's tiny canvas: there are Mondrian's nine modular paintings of 1918–19 (see, for example, fig. 2), a few contemporaneous paintings by Vilmos Huszar, now lost, a few color sketches by Georges Vantongerloo, a few glass assemblages dating from 1922 by Josef Albers, and a few later canvases by Theo van Doesburg.[67] Even Rodchenko's deductive pattern of a series of woodcuts made in 1921 cannot be called plain grids (insofar as he added variety by superimposing circles and oblique lines on the system of modular coordinates).[68] The issue, of course, is not the occurrence of the grid: as with any other pictorial invention, one has to know what to do with it for it to be significant, and from there how to go on. For all these artists (as it would be for Reinhardt in 1940), the grid solution was only a transitional one. Yet for each of them it was a key moment in their struggle against what we could call the arbitrariness of composition (Greenberg's "gift for placing"), against what they called the subjective, the angst, the particular, the natural, the undetermined, the relative (or even, in the case of Rodchenko, the "bourgeois"). The power of the modular grid is that it is at once a deductive (centripetal) structure and an all-over (centrifugal) system. As such, it eliminates any notion of a final formal unity: this unity is a given at the beginning, thus there is no struggle to achieve it; it is not a reward.

For Mondrian and for Rodchenko, to take the two most articulate spokesmen among the artists listed earlier, the grid provided a way out of the "truing and fairing" associated with

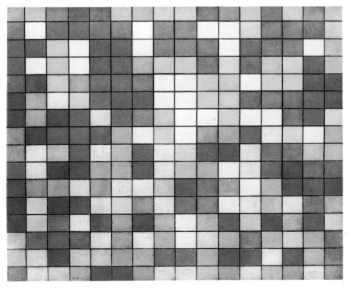

FIG. 2. PIET MONDRIAN. *CHECKERBOARD COMPOSITION IN LIGHT COLORS.* 1919. OIL ON CANVAS, 33¾ × 41¾" (86 × 106 CM). HAAGS GEMEENTEMUSEUM, THE HAGUE, THE NETHERLANDS

Cubism, the *com*-posing, the putting together, the adjusting of heterogeneous fragments into a reconstituted formal and organic unity. It showed negatively the indissoluble link between the "push and pull" qua depth (literal surface versus illusion) and qua extension (the two corners mocked by Stella, the compositional equilibrium). The modular grid completely eliminated the elements to be combined (no more figure, hence no more figure/ground opposition): only two things remained to be asserted, the edge and the extension of the ground as such. Rodchenko's use of the grid led to his monochrome triptych, which signaled his departure from painting, simultaneous with his exploration of modular, deductive, Minimalist, one-thing-next-to-the-other sculptures. These works, in turn, immediately led to his renunciation of art as an autonomous practice. Mondrian, on the contrary, particularly conscious of the fact that the modular grid, by virtue of its indexical nature, was transforming the painting into an object, hence leading toward the death of painting-as-art, decided to back up. It was from this retreat, which took up about a year and a half, that the Neoplastic style was born. But the historicist notion of a "retreat" is not appropriate here, for Mondrian had understood that for all its deductiveness, the grid only seemed to dissolve the arbitrariness he was determined to eradicate: true, the module came about directly from the format of the painting, to which it was proportionate, but then, what about this format itself? In a sense, paradoxically, the grid was even more an a priori projection than the old naturalistic image. It was a pure idea, entirely calculated beforehand, and it did not even need to be materialized. This was a conceptual, that is, easy, victory: if composition was to be destroyed at all in any definitive sense, it had to be through the *membra disjecta* of painting. From then on, these elements (lines, colors, non-colors, verticals, horizontals, planes, position, extension) were conceived of as engaged in a dialectical process in which their task was to cancel out one another. This was Mondrian's concept of composition (which would later be debased in Hofmann's pedagogy).

Despite what he might seem at times, Reinhardt was not a dialectician. Furthermore, he had tried Mondrian's pictorial rhetoric and could see for himself (with the help of the various disasters produced by the A.A.A.) that it was more or less an ad hoc system, unsuitable for use by others. But what his single grid canvas made him understand was that what had to be fought against was not only composition as such—the balances and counterbalances, the relational idea—but also, especially, its a priori character. This meant, first, getting rid of geometry, of projection, getting rid of sketching, getting rid of drawing. That is exactly the function of Reinhardt's collages of 1940, or rather the function they took on after his single grid canvas. As such, they are far from being the "end of something," contrary to what Greenberg thought. The first collages (dating from 1939) are undoubtedly Cubist in character. Ironically, they gradually switch from a Synthetic Cubist organization (see plates, p. 36, top left and right, bottom left) to a facet-like Analytic one (see plate, p. 38, bottom right: its black border emphasizes an analogy with Braque's and Picasso's works of 1910–12). But others are frighteningly all-over, seeming to be arranged almost at random, and above all emphatically cropped at the edge (see fig. 3).[69] The violence of these small works is not so much that the photographs used as raw material are cut into fragments so tiny as not to let their figurative content intrude on the all-over effect (although this fragmentation, initiated in the previous collages, was certainly instrumental in the new conception of the all-over put forward here), but that they could continue ad infinitum. The inextricability of the all-over and of the deductive structure that had been sealed by the grid structure was now cut loose. In this sense, Martin James is absolutely right when he stresses that Reinhardt was the first to produce totally abstract all-over works in America (Mark Tobey's experiments with this date from at least two years later, even if a tendency to overcrowd his figurative works of the thirties shows that he was naturally drawn to it,

albeit from an entirely different point of view).[70]

Until the late forties, according to Reinhardt himself (in fact well into 1950 and occasionally as late as 1952), he explored the all-over structure. When he claimed in 1958 that he had "almost ten years ago, in the late forties, lost interest in this clear and distinct idea, which . . . everyone understands now," one wonders if it was not to dissociate himself from the temporary acceptance of this structure by Greenberg at the time of the "crisis" (1948).[71] It was certainly to dissociate his practice from that of Pollock. And here, it must be said, Greenberg is right to point to Pollock's "variety": for this artist, the issue was not primarily to dispense with Mondrian's dialectical composition, to arrive at a non-differential surface, perhaps not even to bury definitively the figure (there are arresting accents, "eyes in the heat," as it were, in even the most "polyphonic" of Pollock's drip paintings, and an accent necessarily reinstates a figure/ground opposition, even if, or rather especially if, as in the best Pollocks, this opposition is only fleetingly perceived). And this is not only because he arrived at the all-over drip via Surrealism and the whole set of ideological presuppositions surrounding the notion of automatism. To be specific: Pollock's genius in his drip paintings of 1947–50, as Michael Fried has incontrovertibly stated, was to have emancipated line "from the job of describing contours and bounding shapes."[72] But he did it by endowing his skeins of paint with a dynamism that, in itself, because it involves a fictive, perceived movement, disengages them from their material ground (in this sense, dynamism is always figurative).

In fact, when comparing Pollock and Reinhardt, the opposition of dynamic and static is perhaps the most telling one, and Reinhardt's love for the formulaic traditions of art, for the icon, is to be understood in this light. It is paradoxically their dynamism, however surreptitious, that not only prevents Pollock's canvases from being extensible laterally (they are not "apocalyptic wallpaper," although they appeared as such to many at the time)[73] but also determines their orientation. Dynamism implies an anti-gravitational opposition to the vertical and horizontal coordinates provided by the limits of the canvas; it presupposes right and left, top and bottom. Pollock's drip paintings (and Mondrian's New York paintings) are perhaps the least bound to the classic notion of the visual spectacle offered to an erect beholder in the tradition of "easel painting," of composition, but they remain within this tradition nonetheless.[74] The numerous anecdotes about Pollock cropping his paintings after they were finished (very rarely, in fact) or having trouble knowing where to

FIG. 3. AD REINHARDT, *COLLAGE*. 1940.
PASTED NEWSPRINT, 9 × 11" (22.9 × 27.9 CM). PRIVATE COLLECTION

FIG. 4. AD REINHARDT. *UNTITLED.* N.D. GOUACHE ON PAPER, 22½ × 31" (57.2 × 78.7 CM).
WHITNEY MUSEUM OF AMERICAN ART, NEW YORK. 50TH ANNIVERSARY GIFT OF MR. AND MRS. EDWIN A. BERGMAN

sign them just confuse the matter, for both the eventual crop-ping and the signing implied an aesthetic decision about orienta-tion that, once made, was irrevocable (a drip Pollock turned upside down becomes altered dramatically and, sometimes, collapses).

This is not so with Reinhardt's paintings (in this sense *they* are "apocalyptic wallpaper"). In the basement of the Whitney Museum of American Art is an undated gouache from the late forties (see fig. 4), something between the positive/negative, optically flickering statement made by *Untitled (Yellow and White)* and *Untitled (Red and Gray)*, both of 1950 (plates, pp. 52, 53), and what Reinhardt called his "brick paintings" (see, for example, plate, p. 51, and figs. 5, 6, 7). The label on the back reads "orientation not known." This could not have been affixed to the back of a Pollock, not only because of that artist's different attitude toward the signature, but also because, coming from a different world than Reinhardt, Pollock did not feel he had to carry the monism of the surface this far—he did not have to expectorate the Mondrian within himself, so to speak.

The phrase "not this far," however, would imply a difference in degree, not in nature, and I believe the latter is the case. One

of the critical labels that stuck to Reinhardt for a while (although it was dropped after his final show) was that of "Abstract Expres-sionist." As is extremely well known, he resented this affiliation immensely. He became more and more virulent, from 1954 on (that is, from his first diatribe at a College Art Association meet-ing), against the histrionic poses assumed by his alleged col-leagues (he was disgusted by the action painting mythology, but also by the grandiose claims regarding "subject matter"). The structure of this rage (which exceeds all the others in Rein-hardt's angry writings) is worth considering. One example will suffice: many published and unpublished documents attest to the fact that Reinhardt remained fond of Rothko, despite the Houston chapel, the idea of which he found preposterous. Yet we find in his notes: "What's wrong with the art world is not Andy Warhol or Andy Wyeth but Mark Rothko. The corruption of the best is the worst."[75] This is the moral stance of every great satirist: there is no point in denouncing plainly visible cor-ruption, for it is the masks that must be removed (in his first published piece, a short note explaining what he wanted to achieve as an editor of the *Columbia Jester*, a student news-paper at Columbia University, Reinhardt wrote: "We dislike

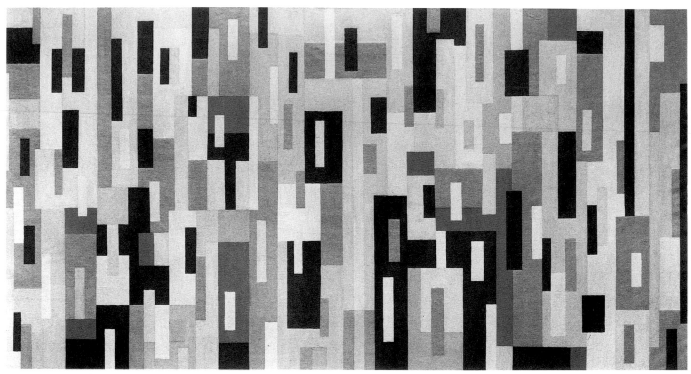

FIG. 5. AD REINHARDT. *ABSTRACT PAINTING.* 1948. WATER- AND OIL-BASED PAINTS, INK ON CANVAS, 76 × 144″ (193 × 365.8 CM).
ALLEN MEMORIAL ART MUSEUM, OBERLIN COLLEGE, OBERLIN, OHIO. RUTH C. ROUSH FUND FOR CONTEMPORARY ART, 1967

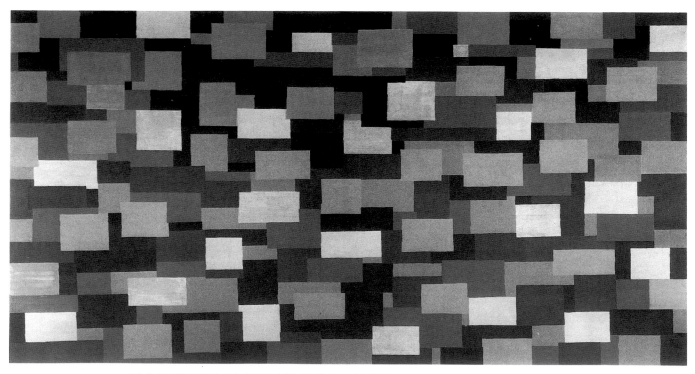

FIG. 6. AD REINHARDT. *NUMBER 88, 1950, BLUE.* 1950. OIL ON CANVAS, 75¼ × 143⅜″ (191.2 × 364.2 CM).
HIRSHHORN MUSEUM AND SCULPTURE GARDEN, SMITHSONIAN INSTITUTION, WASHINGTON, D.C. GIFT OF THE JOSEPH H. HIRSHHORN FOUNDATION, 1972

FIG. 7. AD REINHARDT. *ABSTRACT PAINTING, NO. 2.* 1952.
OIL ON CANVAS. DIMENSIONS AND PRESENT LOCATION UNKNOWN

pseudo-people").[76] Abstract Expressionism represented more and more, for Reinhardt, the beginning of what he called the great "selling out": the confusion this "movement" created between abstraction and Surrealism engendered the subsequent mess (Pop art is seen as a product of this confusion). In the thirties at least, Reinhardt would say over and over (and more and more often toward the end of his life) that there was a clear demarcation between abstraction and Surrealism. (One witnesses a growing nostalgia in Reinhardt's statements: one of his last proposals to *Art News* was an article about Carl Holty, his old A.A.A. professor, and in his late notes one finds nice words about Burgoyne Diller.) It is here that Lucy Lippard's remark holds truest: Reinhardt *was*, in many ways, a painter of the thirties. His moral tone belongs to this period (he even dates his use of the term "selling out" to this time);[77] like Mondrian, who could not stand what he called the "halves" (the semi-abstract painters), Reinhardt had no tolerance for compromises in art. Thus, the term *abstract* "can only make sense in the way the earlier and older abstract artists used it,"[78] that is, as a negative, absolute notion.

Yet the virulence of his attacks against Abstract Expressionist painters implies a deep wound. Reinhardt insists time and again on what separates him from these artists, but he also writes: "Traitor, betrayal. Abstract-expressionists acted as if I were betraying them. But they were betraying me for two decades."[79] In other words, he had been misled, he had thought that they were speaking a common language. This language, I would argue, was what Reinhardt thought to be the new "directness" of painting, the end of sketching and of the compositional a priori, the search for "oneness." Thus he was tempted by Abstract Expressionist calligraphy, by the loosening of the brush, which he saw as a triumph of impersonality, the all-over handwriting as a way of getting rid of all handwritings ("But it was all a getting rid of, and in no instance did I ever make anything of anything. . . . The all-over painting idea, where it's destructive of brush handling and clichés of brush-work and form and figures, is important. . . . At no point, looking back, was I involved in making a business out of anything").[80] That is also the way Clement Greenberg interpreted Pollock's drip technique, although possibly not at the time (his discussion of Pollock's impersonal technique, of the critique of manual dexterity it represents, appeared only in a little-known article of 1967).[81] But even if the action painting myth ("Jack the Dripper," and so on) had not prevented most people from considering Pollock's art in this light, the demagogic Sturm und Drang of Willem de Kooning's zealots was forceful enough to overshadow any other interpretation of Abstract Expressionism until at least the late sixties.[82]

There is no point in tracing in detail the evolution of Reinhardt's art between 1940 and 1950, and it is perfectly consistent with Reinhardt's idea of timelessness that this should be so: his paintings are timeless because they diligently, carefully, assiduously avoid dynamism (the rendition of time in the pictorial order), and as such cannot "evolve" one from the other. Reinhardt himself insisted on this aspect of his art in the choice of illustrations for his parodic "Reinhardt Paints a Picture" (1965) as well as on other occasions: a suite of all-over paintings of the same long vertical format, side by side, dated from 1939 to 1953.[83] One could not even say, for example (I depart here from Margit Rowell's account), that during that time Reinhardt "replays" Mondrian's evolution toward the modular grid (for one thing, Reinhardt begins with the terminal point). He does not even "rewind" it; there is no sequence, hence no real parallel. One can only say that throughout the forties Reinhardt deals with

FIG. 8. PIET MONDRIAN. *COMPOSITION WITH COLOR PLANES, V.* 1917.
OIL ON CANVAS, 19⅜ × 24⅛″ (49.2 × 61.3 CM).
THE MUSEUM OF MODERN ART, NEW YORK.
THE SIDNEY AND HARRIET JANIS COLLECTION

most compositional schemes invented by Mondrian between 1913 and 1919, including again, but this time in a much more subdued way, the modular grid (see *Number 114, 1950*; plate, p. 60). There are what could be called "Cubist-Impressionist" compositions, retracted from the edge, to be linked with, for example, Mondrian's *Composition VII* of 1913, at the Guggenheim Museum: *Number 4* of 1946; *Black and White, 1947*; *Number 43 (Abstract Painting, Yellow)* of 1947 (see plates, pp. 39, 42, 43). Then there are works of a "post-plus-and-minus-Mondrianism, with consistency of deliberate and random repetition of identical elements but without scotch-taping-shifting-balancing-spacing-Cézanneism"[84]: *October*, 1949 (plate, p. 47, left), *Number 22*, 1949 (plate, p. 45, left). Then there is a direct

allusion to the superposed counterpoint of Mondrian's *Composition, 1916* (at the Guggenheim Museum) and to the two works *Composition with Color Planes A* and *B*, from the beginning of 1917: *Red, Green, Blue and Orange*, 1948; *Untitled*, 1949; *Number 5 (Red Wall)*, 1952 (plates, pp. 48, left; 48, right; 61). Then, finally, there are the run-off-the-edge brick compositions, very close to Mondrian's five late-1917 works in which he used what he called his "blocketjes," his "little blocks" (see fig. 8): *Untitled*, 1948; *Blue Painting* of 1950–51; *Abstract Painting* of 1950–51 (plates, pp. 57, 63, 66). The type of canvas that emerged from this long immersion in Mondrian's territory, this long destruction of his push-and-pull oppositions, this long devitalization of the old master's dialectics (art ought to be dead) is best exemplified by *Abstract Painting, Gray* of 1950 (plate, p. 54)—a work that is laterally extensible (limitless), entirely covered with paint (no background), and has no configurations (formless). It is not colorless yet, however: no matter how subdued, the tiny flecks of washed-out blue, green, or yellow still constitute accents.

One could refine the formal analysis and point out instances in which Reinhardt departs radically from the Mondrian model. I would like to insist rather on the subliminal departure, on the way his paintings never look quite like Mondrian's, especially when they look almost subservient to them. This is a problematic issue, for it involves the admission of a certain failure; it involves understanding why those 1940–50 canvases never struck a great chord—but also why they should not have. This is where the difficulty lies. Most critics during the early years, even in the complacent *Art News*, were quick to characterize Reinhardt's works as "decorative" patterns (his ironical nickname of "Persian rugs" for the most color-saturated of these paintings is a direct answer to that charge, yet it is also an indication that something else was at stake). Even Dore Ashton, a great admirer of Reinhardt's "black" canvases, would write in 1960, on the occasion of his retrospective at Betty Parsons, "twenty years of questions and answers in which the questions were never quite right, and five years of the right questions and the absolutely right answer."[85] Although it seems rather harsh, in a sense it is not an incorrect verdict (I only disagree slightly with her chronology, as it leaves out the early fifties, during which important features of Reinhardt's later works—symmetry, monotone—will be searched for, and obtained).

I have already discussed at great length various reasons for Reinhardt's unavailability during his lifetime, and, in doing so, have used Greenberg (and his pet artist, Hofmann) as a foil: I resent having to do that to some extent but see no other way, Greenberg's discourse providing by far the most articulate critical approach of the time. So it is useful to turn again briefly to Greenberg, albeit indirectly, through Morris's complaint. Musing on the attempt of abstraction (of the A.A.A. type) at "depersonalization," Morris wrote: "It was interesting to hear Arp mention this a few months ago: 'I don't want to be *great*—there are too many forces throughout the world today that are *great*.' This was not spoken in modesty; it merely represents a new relation between the artist and his work; we do not need that competition for omnipotence that critics are so intent upon grading, only an impulse than can achieve distinction and sensibility in a fragment."[86] I believe such a statement to be very close to Reinhardt's position (even the analogy, which follows, with the anonymous craftsmen of the Middle Ages: after all, among other things, it is the anonymity and "unoriginality" of Cambodian sculpture or Islamic art that attracted Reinhardt). One can see how this self-effacing desire utterly contradicts Greenberg's constant calling for High, Major, Ambitious art. Reinhardt's program, in many ways, was against greatness. But how does one fulfill it—how, forcefully, not to be great? How does one effectively make "minor" art? (Of course, the term "minor" is inappropriate, but the impossibility of finding an antonym for "major" devoid of deprecating connotations demonstrates the hold that the aesthetic of heroism has on our culture.) Either one advocates the courage of this renunciation (and then it is to be read as yet another gesture, far from anonymous), or—which is precisely what happened to Reinhardt—one's art can only be seen as "decorative."[87]

Despite the fact that he sharply disallowed decorative art as an antecedent for the all-over,[88] Reinhardt maintained an ambiguous position toward it. On the one hand, decorative art was, for him, guilty of the only mortal sin in art: it was not "pure"; it was applied, "used" ("any use is a misuse" could be a catchphrase for Reinhardt's aesthetic, certainly the strongest position in this century against any kind of instrumentalization of art).[89] On the other hand, the term "decorative" was part of a whole set of derogatory qualifications bestowed upon abstract art in the thirties (along with "meaningless," "imageless," "inhuman," "sterile," "cold," "academic," "dogmatic," "empty," "unemotional," "escapist," "formalist," "absolute"). It was ac-

tually the most common slur on abstract art, as any veteran of the A.A.A. can easily recall. As Reinhardt pointed out several times, he strove, in the forties, to invert the negative polarity of all these words: the fact that "decorative" does not figure in the list of "negative" qualities to be retrieved is of course consequent, given his battle against instrumentalization. Yet he was enough of an admirer of Clive Bell's *Art*, his favorite reference ("roughly my point of view"),[90] to know that the metaphor of the Persian carpet was looming on every page of the Bloomsbury pamphlet.

Reinhardt's ambivalence toward the decorative is genuine and typical. His art is not decorative, but almost. Its problem, in the forties, was that Reinhardt had not yet found the way to make this almostness seen: he proposed an understatement to a beholder equipped only for an overstatement; he murmured in ears trained to hear only shouts. It took him a long time to understand that he would first have to transform his auditor, to alter the phenomenological conditions of the perceptibility of his art in such a way that the beholder, at least if he or she were willing to take it even mildly seriously, would have to renounce completely any usual expectations.

The first step in this direction (to make subliminality visible) is the equalization of values and the use of the near-monotone. This is logical, as another example earlier in this century could show: the development of the Polish Constructivist painter Władisław Strzeminski. To understand how Strzeminski had been naturally driven to the near-monotone (then to the mere monochrome, a step that Reinhardt would never have wanted to take), let us recall that the Polish painter's explicit critique of Mondrian was exactly that enacted by Reinhardt implicitly, and that his entire program was, in fact, almost that of Reinhardt: no composition, no contrast, no struggle, no dynamism (see figs. 9, 10).[91] There are, after all, not very many ways to abolish dynamism, figure/ground opposition, and the like. Reinhardt's first attempt at this formal structure (the near-monotone) was infecund, perhaps because it was too early and still unnecessary (the all-over had not been fully explored yet). As a result, it was too assertive to produce the effect of almostness: the white on white was feeble precisely because it was too violently white on white (see *Untitled (White)* of 1945, p. 38, top right). The issue of the non-color reappears, in the early fifties, in connection with the all-over brushstrokes (see *Number 107* of 1950, p.

FIG. 9. WLADISLAW STRZEMINSKI. *COMPOSITION ARCHITECTONIQUE.* 1929.
OIL ON CANVAS, 37¾ × 23⅔ (96 × 60 CM).
MUZEUM SZTUKI, LODZ, POLAND

Drawing had to be reinstated (and geometry was the surest way to accomplish that), but it had to be simultaneously destroyed. The only means not yet explored for this particular purpose was color.

Two options were available to Reinhardt for undermining drawing through color, for rendering the line evanescent while retaining it (something in which Josef Albers was perhaps an ally: we know he felt that Reinhardt's art was close to his at this time, and he invited him to teach at Yale University in 1952–53): either the high pitch, or the low key. The canvases from late 1950 through 1951 (but some as late as 1953) belong to both categories. The whole issue of drawing does not cry out immediately because the monotonal device is first found in conjunction with the all-over "brick" structure (a number of these canvases have been mentioned earlier). Opting for highly saturated color are works like *Number 114* of 1950 (plate, p. 60), *Blue Painting* of 1951 (plate, p. 63), *Number 15, 1952* (plate, p. 64, left), and even the two "Op" works in the Meyerhoff collection (plates, pp. 52, 53). The low key is represented by *Abstract Painting* of 1951 (plate, p. 67) and *Number 17* of 1953 (plate, p. 65). But the problem of drawing becomes instantly apparent

FIG. 10. WLADISLAW STRZEMINSKI. *UNISTIC COMPOSITION 8.* 1931–32.
OIL ON CANVAS, 23½ × 14" (60 × 36 CM).
MUZEUM SZTUKI, LODZ, POLAND

55). Here, Reinhardt immediately perceived the problem (a problem that Strzeminski had discerned in Malevich much earlier): if the issue was to abolish contrast (without arriving at the plain monochrome, objecthood, and the like), then the suppression of colors as a means of dispensing with color-contrast was only a brilliant trick (for textural effects could always be perceived as the sublation of such contrast). To approach it indirectly, by way of value deflation, was much more promising. Paradoxically, to thematize this abolition of contrasts through an attenuation of values, one had to *show* this attenuation and thus reintroduce something abandoned long ago, that is, drawing.

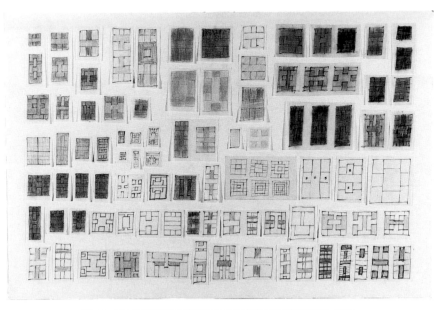

FIG. 11. AD REINHARDT. *PERSONAL SKETCHES OF PAINTINGS.* 1966.
COLORED PENCIL AND INK ON PAPER, MOUNTED ON BOARD,
20⅛ × 30¼" (51.1 × 76.8 CM).
COLLECTION OF MILLY AND ARNE GLIMCHER, NEW YORK

in *Abstract Painting* of 1950 (plate, p. 58), *Abstract Painting* of 1951–52 (plate, p. 59), or *Abstract Painting, Blue, 1953* (plate, p. 64, right).

It is at this juncture that the grid reappears, at least that characteristic of the grid that can be dissociated from its all-overness: its deductive nature. It is also, logically, the moment at which the sketch reappears, at least theoretically (see fig. 11). Strzeminski, who had also adopted the deductive structure as one possible solution to his problem, had managed to avoid the sketch only by using a complex system of proportional relations that had to be planned on the spot (each division of the canvas was made according to the ratio of its length to its width). Furthermore, for a whole set of ideological reasons too complex to be analyzed here, the simplest deductive structure, symmetry, was unavailable to him (for an abstract painter in the twenties, symmetry paradoxically meant composition). But it was indeed available to Reinhardt. (I am not sure that the example of Barnett Newman should necessarily be brought in, if only because Newman's use of symmetry is conspicuously indexical and bilateral, while Reinhardt's is mostly, and after the adoption of the tripartition, exclusively, biaxial.) His sudden recourse to symmetry in the early fifties is a consequence of his "exhaustion" of the all-over scheme: again, there are only so many ways to deal with non-composition.

It seems that the first of Reinhardt's symmetrical canvases was a somewhat emphatically multicolored painting of 1950 (*Untitled*, plate, p. 62). To my mind, this work fails, but a lesson might be drawn from it and was drawn by Reinhardt (even if he had to verify it in a second attempt, this time a much harsher one, two years later in *Red and Blue, 1952* (plate, p. 76, left): symmetry cannot abolish composition if color and value differences are to be reinforced. (What could be done, however, if strong colors were to be used, was the cancellation of their difference by the equalization of both their value and their degree of saturation.) Since Reinhardt knew by then that the suppression of contrast does not alone perform the task of destroying composition without a renewed investigation of drawing, he concluded that only the combination of the two features could provide his painting with the negative force he had in mind.

Reinhardt later found his blue and his red canvases of the early and mid-fifties too attractive. I think he meant they were too assertive, all their difficulties having been thought out during the thirteen preceding years (1940–53). He was, generally speaking, much too hard on himself, but he might have been right: much more than the all-over canvases or the brick paintings of the forties, these works are, today, immediately accessible. At the

27

end of his review of their first public presentation, Tom Hess wrote, "And there is (that terrible word) beauty." Could the battle over agon be won after all? Perhaps this struggle had been the paragon of agonism: was it over? Of course not. But, perhaps, almost. This is a particular feature of Reinhardt's extraordinary system: even when he seems to surrender—to beauty, for instance—it is only almost: only Reinhardt could almost suppress almostness. In the blue and in the red canvases, nothing of what has been noted before—the "minorness," the stillness—has been discarded. But the sheer sensuality of the color of these works keeps those strenuous issues at bay, at least at first glance—and if one manages to sustain one's gaze past that first look, one is already understanding what is specific to Reinhardt; one already "gets" a good part of what his art has to say. Also, those paintings support one another through a serial effect (the series as a sort of extension of the all-over's repetitiousness). Perhaps this explains why I do not feel such an urge to defend them, to protect them from misreadings. The series notion is somewhat misleading in that it incites a comparative search for differences between one canvas and the next (to judge, balance). But how does one speak about them without doing this? I have not found a way yet, although I am confident that I will. The only thing I can say at the moment is that their exploration of color is as innovative as that of Albers: the fictive transformation of one color into two, and vice versa, the modulation of boundaries—soft, hard—through color-neighboring— such are the features on which the quiet beat of these canvases is based. But their allure, perhaps because the color range is more narrow, is less "professorial." These paintings will never become pedagogical exercises. Yet I cannot help seeing them as a patient rehearsal for what is to come, the "black" paintings.

I would have liked, of course, to deal at great length with the "black" canvases, Reinhardt's major achievement. What I have said so far, however, should clarify many issues pertaining to these later works (this is also true, I hope, for the blue and the red canvases about which I have just been so cursory): their triumph is due to the fact that, at last, Reinhardt had found a way to force the spectator to accept his terms. This is why I have been so painstaking in determining the conditions of Reinhardt's reception: if accessibility has been the main problem with Reinhardt's work, it is also because it is the main issue his work had been dealing with all along, in a fundamental way.

For the beholder of a "black" canvas, there are only two choices: either one rushes by and sees nothing, or one spends a few minutes (1958), a quarter of an hour (1960), half an hour (1967) in front of *each* canvas. (With the "black" paintings, the effect is not serial, as in the red or the blue paintings; the differences become so minimal, the necessary adjusting period so long, the engagement with each canvas has to be so total, that there is, physically, no possibility of making comparisons.) And what does one see? At first there is nothing, but gradually, of course, one discerns almost nothing, evanescent entities, phantoms of colors and shapes one can never be quite sure one has seen. Enough commentators (Colt, Ashton, Lippard) have rigorously described their hypnotic experience in front of a "black" Reinhardt. All have insisted on the temporality that is implied: this, I think, is one of the most extraordinary features of Reinhardt's later works.[92] The only way his art managed to exclude time, that is, the illusion of time (dynamism, narration), was to incorporate it into the mode of reception of his work. The only way to achieve timelessness was to fold time back on the spectator: what one sees in front of a "black" Reinhardt is the narrativization of one's gaze (first this bar or that square "appears," but then it dissolves, to be replaced by a similarly waning epiphany, leaving one with one's doubts, a plea: "Wait a minute, don't go away!")[93] The second remarkable feature of these works, alluded to by Martin James, concerns light, and the same structure of reversal applies. Reinhardt, again, is the least optical painter (no push and pull, no shallow depth, no abstract land that the eyes alone can visit), yet at the same time he could be called the *only* such painter. Indeed, he reduces the spectator to the sole organ of his or her vision; he dematerializes the beholder him- or herself, so to speak (yet another instance of his distance from Minimalism). What one then perceives, in the blackest of the "black" paintings, is no longer the infinitesimal variation of color (although of course this plays a part), but the always fleeting, always dubitable, beginning, the promise of a speck of light, the "last vestige of brightness."[94] The two aspects are indissolubly linked: the reward of this timeless instant is only available to those who have faith enough to withstand its infinite duration.

I just spoke of "faith." It is on purpose, for a coda must be added about religion. As his posthumously published notes reveal, Reinhardt was a reader of religious texts, especially the various mystical, oxymoronic traditions that glorified the night, inverting it into light. Yet he also insisted, constantly, on the fact that his art had nothing to do with religion (he found preposterous the idiotic interpretation of his tripartition—that is, a grid on the verge of the figural—as alluding to Christianity). Yet, he admitted once that in a sense religion might be "the best analogy to-day," and indeed what he had wanted to achieve in his art immediately calls to mind "negative theology." This last reference is quite telling, for it concerns the structure of the almost: what Reinhardt means is that his negative language, and art, are naturally condemned to look religious—almost. It almost looks religious because, as does negative theology, it is concerned only with the "not that, but almost." The analogy is thus inevitable, but it is also a confusion. The logic of this confusion has been perfectly analyzed by Jacques Derrida, whose enterprise of deconstruc-

tion has also suffered from it: "As soon as a proposition takes a negative form, it is enough to push the negativity thus announced to its limit, for the proposition to resemble, at least, a theological apophantic. Each time I say: X is neither this nor that, nor the contrary of this or that, nor the simple neutralization of this or that with which it *has nothing in common*—being absolutely heterogeneous or incommensurable with it—I would commence to speak of God, under this name or under another."[95] Negativity has many guises, many turns. Reinhardt is not Zen, not mystic, not agnostic, not dialectic, not even deconstructive—not anything. But almost. *"Painting that is almost possible, almost does not exist, that is not quite known, not quite seen."*[96]

AD REINHARDT, 1966.

NOTES

While writing this essay, it became evident that I would have much more to say about Reinhardt, a discovery that was, in fact, exhilarating. Instead of writing an abstract of my argument, which would have made it psychologically difficult for me to approach it again, I decided to let the ideas run at their own slow pace. This means that I have been far more extensive on Reinhardt's difficult beginnings than on the extraordinary last part of his career—if only because it seemed to me that constant misunderstandings of his beginnings still form a major obstacle to a clear grasp of the end. I naturally intend to go beyond the scope of this essay.

I would like to thank Maria Gough and Harry Cooper for helping me to put these pages into better English; Benjamin Buchloh, Rosalind Krauss, James Leggio, Richard Rand, and William Rubin for their editorial comments; and Stephanie Salomon for her work on the final version of this essay.

1. "The First Paintings," undated, in Barbara Rose, ed., *Art as Art: The Selected Writings of Ad Reinhardt* (New York: Viking Press, 1975), p. 11 (hereafter cited as Rose).
2. Ibid., p. 111.
3. "Imageless Icons," undated, Rose, p. 108.
4. Saussure's and Lévi-Strauss's quotations have become landmarks. It is to be noted that Reinhardt himself refers to a structuralist, Roland Barthes, in "The Artist Is Responsible," undated, Rose, p. 134.
5. Ad Reinhardt, quoted in Jeanne Siegel, "Ad Reinhardt: Art as Art," in *Artwords: Discourses on the 60's and 70's* (Ann Arbor, Mich.: U.M.I. Press, 1985), p. 28.
6. "Twelve Rules for a New Academy," 1957, Rose, pp. 204–5.
7. "The Artist in Search of an Academy, Part II," 1954, Rose, p. 202.
8. "The Role of the Artist," undated, Rose p. 139 (my italics).
9. "Five Stages of Reinhardt's Timeless Stylistic Art-Historical Cycle," 1965, Rose, p. 10. This sentence appears between quotation marks.
10. Lucy Lippard, *Ad Reinhardt* (New York: Harry N. Abrams, 1981), p. 82.
11. This ironical name derives from military vocabulary, "section eleven" being the category affixed to those discharged for insanity or other psycho-social miseries. It evokes somewhat (and capitalizes on) the social marginalization of the avant-garde still prevalent in America during the late fifties.
12. Lawrence Campbell, "Ad Reinhardt," *Art News*, October 1960, p. 12. Martin James, "Today's Artists: Reinhardt," *Portfolio and Art News Annual*, no.3, 190, pp. 48–63, 140–146.
13. Shortly after the exhibition Alfred Barr and James Thrall Soby would publicly defend Reinhardt against an art-world lawyer who accused him of being a "fake and a fraud." See "Letter to the Editor," *Art in America*, October 1963, p. 143.
14. The only well-known artist in the exhibition older than Reinhardt was Richard Lindner, an even more unlikely match, if this sort of thing can be measured.
15. Priscilla Colt, "Notes on Ad Reinhardt," *Art International*, October 1964, pp. 32-34; Barbara Rose, "ABC Art," *Art in America*, October–November 1965 (reprinted in Barbara Rose, *Autocritique* [New York: Weidenfeld & Nicholson, 1988], pp. 55–72.)
16. It was hardly a retrospective since, at Reinhardt's specific insistence, it omitted almost all of the red and the blue canvases and went almost directly from the works of the late forties to the "black" paintings.
17. See Barbara Rose, "The Black Paintings," in *Ad Reinhardt: Black Paintings 1951–1967* (New York: Marlborough Gallery, 1970), pp. 16–22; Dore Ashton, "Notes on Ad Reinhardt's Exhibition," *Arts and Architecture*, January 1967, pp. 4–5, 31.
18. Ad Reinhardt, quoted in Bruce Glaser, "An Interview with Ad Reinhardt," reprinted in Rose, p. 18.
19. The same case should be made about Agnes Martin's participation (the case of Jo Baer is a little different).
20. The best analysis of Conceptual art, and of Reinhardt's importance for it, is to be found in Benjamin Buchloh, "From the Aesthetic of Administration to Institutional Critique (Some Aspects of Conceptual Art 1962–1969)," in *L'Art conceptuel: Une Perspective*, Claude Gintz, ed. (Paris: Musée d'Art Moderne de la Ville de Paris, 1989), pp. 41–53.
21. "Art-as-Art," 1966–67, Rose, p. 74. I am referring to Michael Fried's essay "Art and Objecthood" (1967), reprinted in Gregory Battcock, ed., *Minimal Art* (New York: Dutton, 1968), 116–147. One wonders if Reinhardt's cryptic sentence is not an allusion to Fried's essay, which appeared in June (Reinhardt died at the end of August).
22. Skowhegan lecture (1967), quoted in Lippard, op. cit., p. 184.
23. "Art-as-Art," 1966–67, Rose, p. 75.
24. "An Artist, a Fine Artist or Free-artist," undated, Rose, p. 142.
25. "Art-as-Art," 1962, Rose, p. 55.
26. Ad Reinhardt, quoted in Phylisann Kallick, "An Interview with Ad Reinhardt," *Studio International*, December 1967, p. 272.
27. "The Philadelphia Panel," Irving Sandler and Philip Pavia, eds., *It Is*, Spring 1960, p. 35.
28. Ad Reinhardt, quoted in Glaser, op. cit., in Rose, p. 28.
29. On this point, see my review of Hubert Damisch's *Fenêtre jaune cadmium* in *October*, no. 37, Summer 1986, reprinted in my collection of essays, *Painting as Model* (Cambridge, Mass.: MIT Press, 1991), pp. 245–57. It is not by chance that Damisch would find Reinhardt akin to his model: see his essay on Reinhardt, "Attention: Fragile," in *Art Minimal II: De la surface au plan*, Michel Bourel, ed. (Bordeaux: CAPC, 1987), pp. 11–12.
30. "Ad Reinhardt on His Art," *Studio International*, December 1967, p. 269. A student paper by Reinhardt, dating from 1946, concerns the spiral form in modern architecture. The last cartoon pre-

pared for *PM* but not published was entitled "How to Look at a Spiral." See Tom Hess, *The Art Comics and Satires of Ad Reinhardt* (Düsseldorf–Rome: Kunsthalle Düsseldorf and Marlborough Gallery, 1975).

31. "Art is always dead, and a 'living' art is a deception," "The Philadelphia Panel," op. cit., p. 37.

32. Siegel, op. cit., p. 27.

33. Draft of a letter to Sam Hunter, 1966, in Archives of American Art, New York City. It is true that Reinhardt adds "the Mahayana Mandala, Mi Fei, Ma Yuang, Mu Chi, Monotobe, Masaccio" to his list. On the notion of modernism as an art of "the last painting," see "Painting: The Task of Mourning," in *Painting as Model*, op. cit., pp. 229–44.

34. "Art-as-Art," op. cit., Rose, p. 76.

35. Thomas Mann, *The Story of a Novel* (New York: Alfred A. Knopf, 1961), pp. 73–74. The phrase "masters of voidness" is found in "Oneness," undated, Rose, p. 106. Flaubert is not mentioned among the "masters of voidness," but his name appears often in Reinhardt's unpublished notes, as do the names of James Joyce and Lewis Carroll. The reference to Mann is found in "Art-as-Art", 1966–67, op. cit., Rose, pp. 73–74. Hubert Damisch proposed a structuralist reading of Mann's diary entry in "L'autre inquisition," in *Ruptures Cultures* (Paris: Editions de Minuit, 1976), pp. 93–98.

36. "No chess-playing" is the twelfth "Rule for a New Academy," Rose, p. 206.

37. "The Philadelphia Panel," op. cit., p. 35.

38. "Creation as Content," undated, Rose, p. 191.

39. Joseph Kosuth, "Art after Philosophy" (1969). Reprinted in Gregory Battcock, ed., *Idea Art* (New York: Dutton, 1973), p. 78.

40. "Modernist Painting" first appeared in *Arts Yearbook*, no. 4, (1961), pp. 103–8, but remained somewhat confidential until it was reprinted in Gregory Battcock's anthology, *The New Art* (New York: Dutton, 1966). "After Abstract Expressionism" appeared in *Art International*, vol. 6, no. 8 (October 1962), pp. 24–32.

41. Thierry de Duve, "The Monochrome and the Blank Canvas," in *Reconstructing Modernism*, Serge Guilbaut, ed. (Cambridge, Mass.: MIT Press, 1990), pp. 244–310.

42. Clement Greenberg, "After Abstract Expressionism," op. cit., p. 30. This is the most famous statement in Greenberg's essay, and it has often been discussed by other critics. For Michael Fried's comment, see "Art and Objecthood," op. cit., p. 123, note 4.

43. Allan Kaprow, "The Legacy of Jackson Pollock," *Art News*, October 1958, pp. 26–28, 55–57.

44. The affinities between the "black" canvases of the two painters, often noted, are purely illusory (as morphological affinities are most of the time). That Stella bought a "black" painting by Reinhardt as early as 1960, that this was known, and that he later contributed a eulogy to a memorial issue of *artscanada* published just after the death of the painter, undoubtedly reinforced the illusion (see "A Tribute to Ad Reinhardt," *artscanada*, October 1967, p. 19).

45. This appears as early as in the essay "Avant-Garde and Kitsch," in which Hofmann is credited for the (more-than-banal) idea that modernist art is that which is attentive to its medium. See John O'Brian, ed., *Clement Greenberg: Perceptions and Judgments—The Collected Essays and Criticism* vol. I (Chicago: University of Chicago Press, 1986), p. 9.

46. "Review of an Exhibition of Hans Hofmann and a Reconsideration of Mondrian's Theories," in John O'Brian, ed., *Clement Greenberg: Arrogant Purpose—The Collected Essays and Criticism*, vol. 2 (Chicago: University of Chicago Press, 1986), p. 18.

47. "The Present Prospects of American Painting and Sculpture," in O'Brian, ed., *Clement Greenberg: Arrogant Purpose,* op. cit., p. 169.

48. Clement Greenberg, "New York Painting Only Yesterday," *Art News*, Summer 1957, p. 85.

49. Ibid, p. 84.

50. Clement Greenberg, "Hans Hofmann: Grand Old Rebel," *Art News*, January 1959, p. 28.

51. "After Abstract Expressionism," op. cit., p. 24 (my italics).

52. "The Decline of Cubism" in O'Brian, ed., *Clement Greenberg: Arrogant Purpose*, op. cit., p. 212.

53. G.L.K. Morris, "On Critics and Greenberg: A Communication," *Partisan Review*, June 1948, p. 683.

54. "Reply to George L. K. Morris," O'Brian, ed., *Clement Greenberg: Arrogant Purpose*, op. cit., pp. 244–45.

55. "Review of the Exhibition 'Collage,'" op. cit., pp. 260-261.

56. "The Present Prospects of American Painting and Sculpture," in O'Brian, ed., *Clement Greenberg: Arrogant Purpose*, op. cit., p. 166. See also "Review of Exhibitions of Worden Day, Carl Holty, and Jackson Pollock," p. 202, where Pollock's *Cathedral* (1947) is compared to "Picasso's and Braque's masterpieces of the 1912–1915 phase of cubism."

57. Clement Greenberg, "The Jackson Pollock Market Soars," *Sunday New York Times Magazine*, April 16, 1961, p. 132.

58. See "Review of an Exhibition of Karl Knaths and of the Whitney Annual," in O'Brian, ed., *Clement Greenberg: Arrogant Purpose*, op. cit., p.198, for example. François-Marc Gagnon, "The Work and Its Grip," in *Jackson Pollock: Questions* (Montreal: Musée d'Art Contemporain, 1979), pp. 16–42. (Gagnon thinks that Greenberg's early references to Synthetic Cubism are a slip of the tongue; I disagree.)

59. See "Review of Exhibitions of Gaston Lachaise and Henry Moore," O'Brian, ed., *Clement Greenberg: Arrogant Purpose*, op. cit., p. 125.

60. "The Crisis of the Easel Picture," op. cit., p. 223.

61. "Review of Exhibitions of Adolph Gottlieb, Jackson Pollock and Josef Albers, idem, p. 286. On the issue of Greenberg's profound difficulty with the all-over, I benefited greatly from my discussions with Harry Cooper.

62. Clement Greenberg, "Recentness of Sculpture" (1967), reprinted in *Minimal Art*, op. cit., p. 184.

63. Clement Greenberg, "The Late Thirties in New York," *Art and Culture* (Boston: Beacon Press, 1962), p. 230. This essay is a new version of "New York Painting Only Yesterday," mentioned above. The passage in which this sentence appears concerns the gradual depoliticization of art in America after the thirties. I dropped only the word "heroically," which does not apply to Reinhardt; we

31

shall see why later on.

64. See Margit Rowell, *Ad Reinhardt and Color* (New York: Solomon R. Guggenheim Museum, 1980) for the Mondrian/Reinhardt issue.

65. The modular grid had long been one of the pattern structures of applied art (for example in the tradition of quilts), but this has absolutely nothing to do with its introduction into the realm of easel painting. For this reason, I am not certain that Man Ray's bedspread of 1911, pompously entitled *Tapestry* by Roland Penrose, shows any kind of precociousness on the part of its maker (undoubtedly modular, it is no less undoubtedly a quilt, made of rectangular pieces of cloth sewn together). See Roland Penrose, *Man Ray* (Boston: New York Graphic Society, 1975), p. 22 (ill. p. 25). I thank Benjamin Buchloh for this reference. Other examples of the modular grid in decorative art abound in this century: see, for example, Theo van Doesburg and Vilmos Huszar's stained-glass windows. The fact that their exploration of the modular grid in the realm of applied arts preceded their use of it in painting should not lead to confusion between those two domains.

66. See Rosalind Krauss, "Grids," in *The Originality of the Avant-Garde and Other Modernist Myths* (Cambridge, Mass.: MIT Press, 1985), pp. 9–22.

67. Van Doesburg also used a modular grid for his abstract interior design of the Strasbourg café "L'Aubette," in 1927–28. Sophie Taeuber-Arp's design for the same café (as well as the related canvases) present a special case: the grid motif is modular, but it is centered and separated from the edge of the ceiling or wall (or painting) by a wide margin. Furthermore, the proportions of the module have nothing to do with those of the support: thus none of those works are modular as a whole.

68. For an example of these works, see Selim O. Kahn-Magomedov, *Rodchenko: The Complete Works* (Cambridge, Mass.: MIT Press, 1987), p. 76.

69. Besides the work illustrated in the present volume, see the one reproduced in Lippard, op. cit., p. 34, whose all-over-ness is accentuated by the fact that it is made of engravings (hatchings being patterns). Maude Riley noted in her review of Reinhardt's collages and gouaches exhibition in February 1944 (at the Artist's Gallery, New York) that Mondrian, who must have seen them before the show (he died that same month), particularly admired one collage. See Maude Riley, "Fifty-Seventh Street in Review," *Art Digest*, February 15, 1944, p. 20. Although it is certain it is neither one of those two mentioned here (Riley describes it as very colorful), I would not be surprised if Mondrian had chosen one of the same kind: his last works, done in New York, mark a return to the problematic of the all-over that he had abandoned in 1920. In the same manner, it is known that he played a major role in Peggy Guggenheim's decision to support Pollock.

70. Martin James, op. cit., p. 55.

71. "A Contribution to a Journal of Some Future Art Historian," 1958, Rose, p. 9.

72. Michael Fried, *Three American Painters* (Cambridge, Mass.: Fogg Art Museum, 1965), p. 14.

73. The phrase is Harold Rosenberg's, from his famous article "The American Action Painters," *Art News*, vol. 51, no. 5 (September 1952). The essay was severely criticized by Clement Greenberg in "How Art Writing Earns Its Bad Name," *Encounter*, vol. 19, no. 6 (December 1962), pp. 67–71. Pollock's all-over paintings looked like wallpaper (or decorative design) to many at the time of their completion: see for example the "Round Table on Modern Art" published by *Life* (October 11, 1948) in which his *Cathedral* is discussed. Quoted in Francis V. O'Connor, *Jackson Pollock* (New York: The Museum of Modern Art, 1967), p. 44.

74. For a discussion of this issue, see "Mondrian: New York City," in *Painting as Model*, op. cit., pp. 157–83.

75. "Religious Strength Through Market-Place Joy," undated, Rose, p. 190.

76. "Editaurus," *Columbia Jester*, September 1935, p. 9.

77. Ad Reinhardt quoted in Glaser, op. cit., Rose, p. 15.

78. "The Philadelphia Panel," op. cit., p. 35.

79. "Government and the Arts," undated, Rose, p. 180.

80. Ad Reinhardt quoted in Glaser, op. cit., Rose, p. 21.

81. Clement Greenberg, "Jackson Pollock: 'Inspiration, Vision, Intuitive Decision,'" *Vogue* (April 1, 1967), pp. 160–61.

82. Aside from Greenberg's attack on Rosenberg's position, the first major assessment of Pollock to denounce the "expressionist" mythology is the first installment of William Rubin's series of four articles on the painter ("Jackson Pollock and the Modern Tradition," *Artforum*, vol. 5, no. 6 [February 1967], pp. 14–22).

83. The auto-interview (Rose, pp. 11–12) is a parody of the famous series "X paints a picture," in *Art News*, and an answer of sorts to "Mr. Pure Paints a Painting," published in the same series (1958), in which Elaine de Kooning had invented a fictional character caricaturing Reinhardt.

84. "A Contribution to a Journal . . .", op. cit., Rose, p. 9.

85. Dore Ashton, "Art," *Arts and Architecture*, December 1960, p. 4.

86. Morris, op. cit., p. 685.

87. The history of the term "decorative" could be discussed at great length. As is well known, after the Nabis it was used mainly as a synonym for silly prettiness, when applied to painting, by avant-garde artists of this century. The major exception was Matisse, who was perhaps alone in giving the term a definitely positive, if idiosyncratic, meaning. As a shortcut, I refer to it here in the usual pejorative sense.

88. "A Contribution to a Journal . . .," op. cit., Rose, p. 9. This "contribution" was first delivered at a panel on the all-over at which Elaine de Kooning, the first speaker (the second one was Martin James) had declared it "all over" and satirized it as "Mama's-boy art," related to home-sweet-home comfort, decorativeness, and hence (topos of nineteenth-century art criticism) femininity (*It Is*, no. 2 [Autumn 1958], p. 72).

89. "Art-as-Art," op. cit., Rose, p. 76.

90. "Ad Reinhardt on his art," op. cit., p. 265. In Reinhardt's notes, one finds this strange sentence: "Highest art is decorative," followed by an arrow (such a sign indicates, generally, that the fragment so marked has been used in a published essay—which is not the case

here). One cannot determine from the context of these notes if the statement must be taken in earnest, which would be surprising but also very much in the vein of Bell and Fry, or if it is ironic, which would be more in accordance with Reinhardt's other essays. At any rate, this ambiguity could be taken as a sign of Reinhardt's ambivalence toward the decorative (see "Art in the World," undated, Rose, p. 134).

91. For a discussion of Strzeminski, see "Strzeminski and Kobro: In Search of Motivation," in *Painting as Model*, op. cit., pp. 123–55. Strzeminski remains for me the most intelligent theoretician of the first wave of abstract art, but unfortunately far from its best practitioner.

92. This is certainly the one feature that Reinhardt's late works share with Minimalism (albeit for entirely different reasons). An analysis of the issue of instantaneity and its various theoretical ramifications (oneness, Kantian beauty versus Kantian sublime, consciousness) would require too long a development here, especially since it is impossible to draw a clear-cut line. Suffice it to say that for Clement Greenberg (and Michael Fried), the accessibility of a work of art "at a glance" had become, by the mid-sixties, a criterion of a work's quality, but that many artists who rebelled against an agonistic aesthetic (for example, Barnett Newman) spoke about this instantaneity as one of the means to escape composition, relations, and equilibrium.

93. Nothing seems to express better one's experience of a "black" painting than the famous poem in Baudelaire's *Fleurs du Mal*, "A une passante" ["To a Passerby"], especially its third stanza:

Un éclair . . . puis la nuit!—Fugitive beauté
Dont le regard m'a fait soudainement renaître,
Ne te verrai–je plus que dans l'éternité

[A flash . . . then night!—O lovely fugitive,
I am suddenly reborn from your swift glance;
Shall I never see you till eternity?]

(translated by C.F. MacIntyre, in Charles Baudelaire, *The Flowers of Evil*, selected and edited by Marthiel and Jackson Mathews [Norfolk, Conn.: New Directions, 1962], p. 118.)

In his famous reading of this poem, both in "The Paris of the Second Empire in Baudelaire" (1938) and "Some Motifs in Baudelaire" (1939), Walter Benjamin associates the fleeting evanescence of the passerby, via a comparison with Edgar Allan Poe's short story "The Man of the Crowd," to the very experience of modernity. One of the profound reasons for the success of Reinhardt's later works might be that they imply a similar reflection on our lives.

94. "Art-as-Art," op. cit., Rose, p. 73.

95. Jacques Derrida, "Comment ne pas parler," in *Psyché: Inventions de l'autre* (Paris: Galilée, 1987), p. 538. I want to thank Richard Rand for his help on the translation of this passage. For a discussion of the oxymoronic logic of agnosticism, which interested Georges Bataille, see Denis Hollier, "La Nuit américaine," in *Poétique*, no. 22, 1975, pp. 227–43.

96. "Imageless Icons," op. cit., Rose, p. 109. Here I want to pay tribute to Dore Ashton, who wrote in her 1967 review: "In the 'almost' lies his art," op. cit., p. 4.

PLATES

The dating of Ad Reinhardt's work presents particular problems. The organizers of the exhibition were very fortunate to have the assistance of Lucy Lippard, who, having written extensively and authoritatively on Reinhardt, kindly agreed to consult with them on this matter.

Reinhardt generally dated his paintings on the verso when they left his studio, usually just before he sent them to an exhibition. Often, paintings must have been dated months, or even years, after he actually completed work on them. Although he exhibited regularly at the Betty Parsons Gallery, like most artists of his generation he sold few pictures. When unsold works were returned to his studio, he frequently repainted the canvases (after varying amounts of time) in the manner in which he was then working. It is entirely possible, especially with paintings that remained in his possession, that the versos of some canvases bear the dates of the earlier pictures, rather than of the ones painted over them. In the case of the especially fragile "black" paintings of the middle and late fifties and sixties, Reinhardt often found himself restoring works that had long since left his studio. His method was simply to repaint them and, in the process, he sometimes changed them substantially. A number of these pictures have inscribed dates that indicate that they were executed in two campaigns (e.g., 1954–59), but it is likely that others were also repainted though their dates do not reflect this fact.

In the plate section, dates are treated as secure for works that are documented in publications prepared with the artist's cooperation, if the same date also appears on the verso of the painting in the artist's hand. All other dates are considered—to varying degrees—less firm, and they appear in parentheses in the captions.

In addition to the date of the work, Reinhardt also inscribed titles on the versos of his paintings. Over the years many of these titles, which describe the works in nonmetaphorical terms (e.g., *Abstract Painting, 60 × 60", 1965*), have been shortened or changed. Wherever possible, with paintings that retain their original, inscribed backs, Reinhardt's titles have been reinstated in this book.

COLLAGE. 1939. PAPER COLLAGE, 9½ × 13¼" (24.1 × 33.7 CM).
COLLECTION MR. AND MRS. GILBERT H. KINNEY

UNTITLED. (1939). PAPER COLLAGE, 3¾ × 4⅛" (9.5 × 10.4 CM).
COLLECTION MR. AND MRS. CHARLES M. DIKER

COLLAGE. 1939. PAPER COLLAGE, 7 × 9½" (17.8 × 24.1 CM).
COLLECTION MR. AND MRS. CHARLES M. DIKER

COLLAGE. 1940. CUT AND PASTED PAPERS ON CARDBOARD,
15¾ × 13⅛" (40 × 33.3 CM).
THE MUSEUM OF MODERN ART, NEW YORK. GIFT OF THE ARTIST

NUMBER 30. 1938. OIL ON CANVAS, 40½ × 42½″ (102.9 × 107.9 CM).
PRIVATE COLLECTION, ON EXTENDED LOAN TO THE WHITNEY MUSEUM OF AMERICAN ART, NEW YORK

ABSTRACT PAINTING. (1940). OIL ON CANVAS, 15 × 15" (38.1 × 38.1 CM).
PRIVATE COLLECTION

UNTITLED (WHITE). (1945). OIL ON PANEL, 17⅞ × 23¹⁵⁄₁₆" (45.4 × 60.8 CM).
COLLECTION MR. AND MRS. GILBERT H. KINNEY

NEWSPRINT COLLAGE. (1940).
CUT AND PASTED PAPERS ON CARDBOARD, 16 × 20" (40.6 × 50.8 CM).
THE MUSEUM OF MODERN ART, NEW YORK. GIFT OF THE ARTIST

NUMBER 4. (1946). OIL ON CANVAS, 50 × 20″ (127 × 50.8 CM).
PRIVATE COLLECTION, SWITZERLAND

NO. 7. (1949). GOUACHE ON PAPER, 22⅜ × 31⅝" (56.8 × 80.3 CM).
YALE UNIVERSITY ART GALLERY, NEW HAVEN, CONNECTICUT. THE KATHARINE ORDWAY COLLECTION

NUMBER 11. (1950). GOUACHE ON PAPER, 22⁹/₁₆ × 30⅞" (57.3 × 78.4 CM).
COURTESY THE PACE GALLERY, NEW YORK

NUMBER 18, 1948–49. (1948–49). OIL ON CANVAS, 40 × 60″ (101.6 × 152.4 CM).
WHITNEY MUSEUM OF AMERICAN ART, NEW YORK. PURCHASE, 53.13

NUMBER 43 (ABSTRACT PAINTING, YELLOW). 1947. OIL ON CANVAS, 40⅛ × 32″ (101.9 × 81.3 CM).
THE MUSEUM OF MODERN ART, NEW YORK. GIVEN ANONYMOUSLY

BLACK & WHITE, 1947. 1947. OIL ON CANVAS, 60 × 40" (152.4 × 101.6 CM).
THE ART INSTITUTE OF CHICAGO. RESTRICTED GIFT OF DR. AND MRS. EDWIN J. DECOSTA
AND THE WALTER E. HELLER FOUNDATION, 1981.76

Untitled. (1947). OIL ON CANVAS, 40 × 32″ (101.6 × 81.3 CM).
NATIONAL GALLERY OF ART, WASHINGTON, D.C. AILSA MELLON BRUCE FUND AND
GIFT OF THE CIRCLE OF THE NATIONAL GALLERY OF ART, 1988.60.1

NUMBER 22. (1949). OIL ON CANVAS, 50 × 20″ (127 × 50.8 CM).
THE MUSEUM OF MODERN ART, NEW YORK. GIVEN ANONYMOUSLY

NUMBER 16. (1947). OIL ON CANVAS, 50 × 20″ (127 × 50.8 CM).
COLLECTION JOAN AND FRED NICHOLAS

UNTITLED. (C. 1950).
OIL ON CANVAS, 15 × 12″ (38.1 × 30.5 CM).
PRIVATE COLLECTION, SWITZERLAND

UNTITLED. (1948). OIL ON CANVAS, 50 × 20″ (127 × 50.8 CM).
PRIVATE COLLECTION, SWITZERLAND

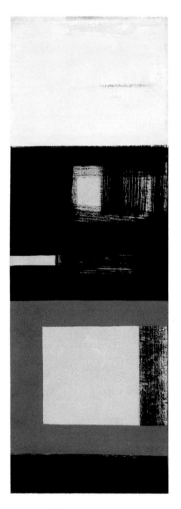

UNTITLED. 1950.
OIL ON CANVAS, 36 × 12″ (91.4 × 30.5 CM).
PRIVATE COLLECTION, SWITZERLAND

OCTOBER. (1949). OIL ON CANVAS, 50⅛ × 20″ (127.3 × 50.8 CM).
COLLECTION MR. AND MRS. GILBERT H. KINNEY

CALLIGRAPHIC PAINTING, 1949–50. (1949–50).
OIL ON CANVAS, 50 × 20″ (127 × 50.8 CM).
PRIVATE COLLECTION, SWITZERLAND

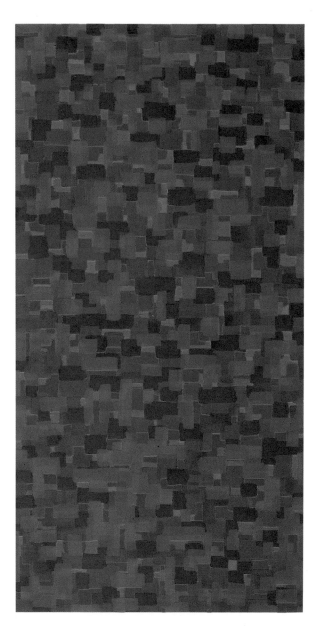

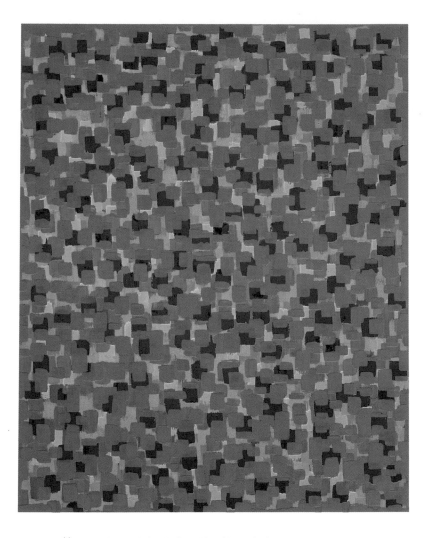

UNTITLED. (C. 1949). OIL ON CANVAS, 40½ × 32½″ (102.9 × 82.5 CM).
PRIVATE COLLECTION, SWITZERLAND

RED, GREEN, BLUE AND ORANGE. (C. 1948).
OIL ON CANVAS, 60 × 29¾″ (152.4 × 75.6 CM).
COLLECTION MR. AND MRS. GILBERT H. KINNEY

NUMBER 111. (1949). OIL ON CANVAS, 60 × 40⅛" (152.4 × 101.8 CM).
THE MUSEUM OF MODERN ART, NEW YORK. GIVEN ANONYMOUSLY

UNTITLED. (C. 1950–51). GOUACHE AND WATERCOLOR ON PAPER, 27½ × 40½″ (69.9 × 102.9 CM).
COLLECTION DENISE AND ANDREW SAUL

UNTITLED. (1950). GOUACHE ON PAPER, 27¼ × 40¼″ (69.2 × 102.2 CM).
THE MONTCLAIR ART MUSEUM, NEW JERSEY. 75TH ANNIVERSARY ACQUISITION MADE POSSIBLE
THROUGH THE BEQUEST OF MRS. FRANK L. BABBOTT, BY EXCHANGE

BRICK PAINTING. (1950). OIL ON CANVAS, 60 × 40″ (152.4 × 101.6 CM).
MANNY SILVERMAN GALLERY, LOS ANGELES

52

UNTITLED (YELLOW AND WHITE). (1950). OIL ON CANVAS, 80 × 60″ (203.2 × 152.4 CM).
COLLECTION ROBERT AND JANE MEYERHOFF, PHOENIX, MARYLAND

UNTITLED (RED AND GRAY). (1950). OIL ON CANVAS, 80 × 60" (203.2 × 152.4 CM).
COLLECTION ROBERT AND JANE MEYERHOFF, PHOENIX, MARYLAND

ABSTRACT PAINTING, GRAY. 1950. OIL ON CANVAS, 30 × 40″ (76.2 × 101.6 CM).
THE METROPOLITAN MUSEUM OF ART, NEW YORK. GIFT OF HENRY GELDZAHLER, 1976 (1976.352)

NUMBER 107. 1950. OIL ON CANVAS, 80 × 36″ (203.2 × 91.5 CM).
THE MUSEUM OF MODERN ART, NEW YORK. GIVEN ANONYMOUSLY

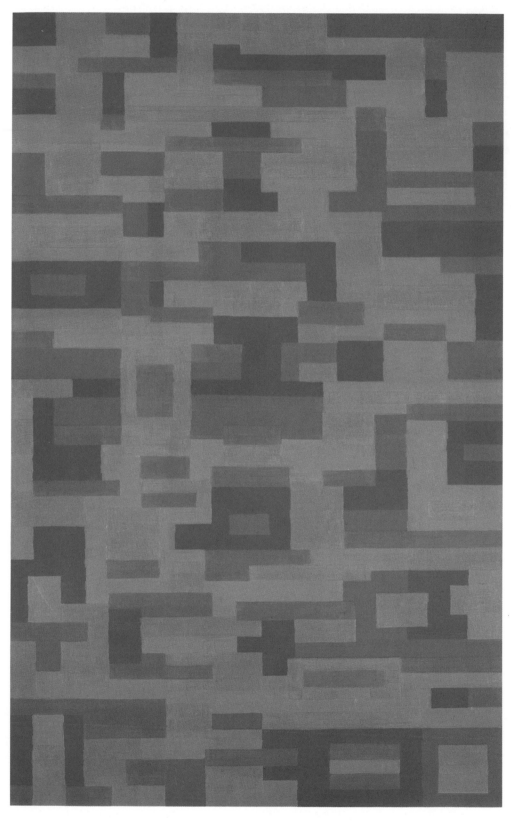

BLUE-GREEN PAINTING, 80 × 50, 1948. (1948). OIL ON CANVAS, 80 × 50″ (203.2 × 127 CM).
COLLECTION MR. AND MRS. GILBERT H. KINNEY

UNTITLED. (1948). OIL ON CANVAS, 60 × 40" (152.4 × 101.6 CM).
PRIVATE COLLECTION

ABSTRACT PAINTING. 1950. OIL ON CANVAS, 60 × 40″ (152.4 × 101.6 CM).
EDWARD TYLER NAHEM FINE ART, NEW YORK

ABSTRACT PAINTING. (C. 1951–52). OIL ON CANVAS, 80 × 42″ (203.2 × 106.7 CM).
TATE GALLERY, LONDON

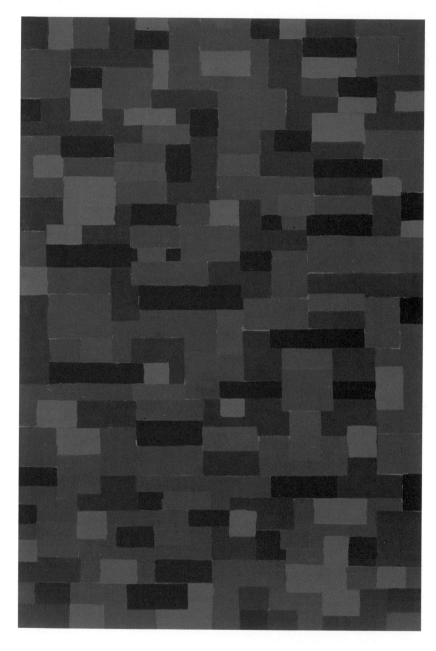

NUMBER 114, 1950. (1950). OIL ON CANVAS, 60 × 40⅛″ (152.4 × 102 CM).
COLLECTION ANNE AND JOEL EHRENKRANZ

NUMBER 5 (RED WALL, 1952). (1952). OIL ON CANVAS, 80 × 42" (203.2 × 106.7 CM).
THE CORCORAN GALLERY OF ART, WASHINGTON, D.C. GIFT OF GILBERT H. KINNEY, 1987.31

UNTITLED. (1950). OIL ON CANVAS, 60⅛ × 18¹⁄₁₆″ (152.7 × 47.3 CM).
COLLECTION MR. AND MRS. GILBERT H. KINNEY

BLUE PAINTING. (1951). OIL ON CANVAS, 87 × 36″ (221 × 91.4 CM).
COLLECTION WILLIAM GREENSPON, NEW YORK

NUMBER 15, 1952. (1952). OIL ON CANVAS, 108¼ × 40¼″ (275 × 102.2 CM).
ALBRIGHT-KNOX ART GALLERY, BUFFALO, NEW YORK. GIFT OF SEYMOUR H. KNOX, 1958

ABSTRACT PAINTING, BLUE. (1953).
OIL ON CANVAS, 108¼ × 40⅛″ (275 × 102 CM).
THE MUSEUM OF MODERN ART, NEW YORK.
GIVEN ANONYMOUSLY (BY EXCHANGE) AND PURCHASE

NUMBER 17. (1953). OIL ON CANVAS, 77¾ × 77¾" (197.5 × 197.5 CM).
WHITNEY MUSEUM OF AMERICAN ART, NEW YORK. PURCHASE. 55.36

ABSTRACT PAINTING, 1950–51. (1950–51).
OIL AND ACRYLIC ON CANVAS, 78 × 24″ (198.1 × 61 CM).
LANNAN FOUNDATION, LOS ANGELES

ABSTRACT PAINTING. (1951). OIL ON CANVAS, 108 × 40″ (274.3 × 101.6 CM).
COLLECTION ROBERT AND JANE MEYERHOFF, PHOENIX, MARYLAND

ABSTRACT PAINTING. (1951). OIL ON CANVAS, 60 × 22″ (152.4 × 55.9 CM).
COLLECTION JESSE PHILIPS

ABSTRACT PAINTING, 1952. 1952.
OIL AND ACRYLIC ON CANVAS, 75 × 28″ (190.5 × 71.1 CM).
THE CARNEGIE MUSEUM OF ART, PITTSBURGH.
GIFT OF THE WOMEN'S COMMITTEE OF THE MUSEUM OF ART, 1965

ABSTRACT PAINTING, RED. (1952).
OIL ON CANVAS, 30 × 15″ (76.2 × 38.1 CM).
COURTESY THE PACE GALLERY, NEW YORK

ABSTRACT PAINTING, RED, 1952. (1952).
OIL ON CANVAS, 50 × 20″ (127 × 50.8 CM).
COURTESY THE PACE GALLERY, NEW YORK

ABSTRACT PAINTING, RED, 1952. (1952). OIL ON CANVAS, 107⅞ × 40″ (273 × 101.6 CM).
THE MUSEUM OF MODERN ART, NEW YORK. PROMISED GIFT OF MR. AND MRS. GIFFORD PHILLIPS

ABSTRACT PAINTING, RED, 1952. 1952. OIL ON CANVAS, 60 × 39⅞″ (152.4 × 101.3 CM).
YALE UNIVERSITY ART GALLERY, NEW HAVEN, CONNECTICUT. GIFT OF THE WOODWARD FOUNDATION

Red Painting, 1952. (1952). OIL ON CANVAS, 60 × 82″ (152.4 × 208.3 CM).
THE VIRGINIA MUSEUM OF FINE ARTS, RICHMOND. GIFT OF SYDNEY AND FRANCES LEWIS, 85.434

RED PAINTING. (1952). OIL ON CANVAS, 78 × 144″ (198.1 × 365.8 CM).
THE METROPOLITAN MUSEUM OF ART, NEW YORK. ARTHUR HOPPOCK HEARN FUND, 1968. (68.85)

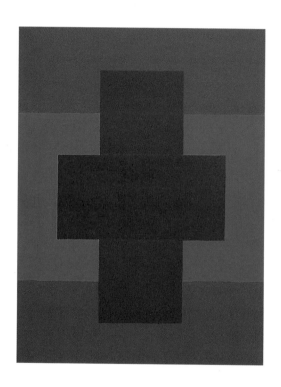

RED AND BLUE, 1952. (1952).
OIL ON CANVAS, 16 × 12″ (40.6 × 30.5 CM).
PRIVATE COLLECTION

ABSTRACT PAINTING, BLUE, 1953. (1953). OIL ON CANVAS, 20 × 16″ (50.8 × 40.6 CM).
YALE UNIVERSITY ART GALLERY, NEW HAVEN, CONNECTICUT.
GIFT OF THE WOODWARD FOUNDATION

BLUE PAINTING. (1953). OIL ON CANVAS, 80 × 60″ (203.2 × 152.4 CM).
COLLECTION WILLIAM GREENSPON, NEW YORK

ABSTRACT PAINTING 6, BLUE, 1952. (1952). OIL ON CANVAS, 30 × 25″ (76.2 × 63.5 CM).
COLLECTION MR. AND MRS. JOHN MARTIN SHEA

ABSTRACT PAINTING, BLUE.
(1953). OIL ON CANVAS,
20 × 10″ (50.8 × 25.4 CM).
COURTESY
THE PACE GALLERY, NEW YORK

ABSTRACT PAINTING, BLUE, 1953.
(1953). OIL ON CANVAS,
20 × 9⅞″ (50.8 × 25.1 CM).
COLLECTION
MR. AND MRS. GILBERT H. KINNEY

ABSTRACT PAINTING, BLUE. (1952).
OIL ON CANVAS,
30 × 10″ (76.2 × 25.4 CM).
COURTESY THE PACE GALLERY, NEW YORK

ABSTRACT PAINTING, BLUE. (1952).
OIL ON CANVAS,
48 × 12″ (121.9 × 30.5 CM).
THE OLIVER-HOFFMANN COLLECTION

ABSTRACT PAINTING, BLUE, 1952. (1952).
OIL ON CANVAS, 60 × 22″ (152.4 × 55.9 CM).
COLLECTION MR. AND MRS. FRANCIS K. LLOYD

ABSTRACT PAINTING, BLUE, 1953. (1953).
OIL ON CANVAS, 50⅛ × 25⅛″ (127.3 × 63.8 CM).
COLLECTION MR. AND MRS. GILBERT H. KINNEY

ABSTRACT PAINTING, BLUE, 1953. (1953).
OIL ON CANVAS, 56 × 22″ (142.2 × 55.9 CM).
COLLECTION MR. AND MRS. CHARLES M. DIKER

ABSTRACT PAINTING, BLUE, 1953. (1953).
OIL ON CANVAS, 50 × 28″ (127 × 71.1 CM).
WHITNEY MUSEUM OF AMERICAN ART, NEW YORK.
GIFT OF SUSAN MORSE HILLES, 74.22

ABSTRACT PAINTING, BLUE, 1953. (1953). OIL ON CANVAS, 30 × 30″ (76.2 × 76.2 CM).
COLLECTION MR. AND MRS. CHARLES H. CARPENTER, JR.

RED PAINTING. (1953). OIL ON CANVAS, 30 × 30″ (76.2 × 76.2 CM).
COLLECTION MARCIA S. WEISMAN

ABSTRACT PAINTING, BLUE, 1953. (1953). OIL ON CANVAS, 50 × 25″ (127 × 63.5 CM).
COLLECTION MILLY AND ARNE GLIMCHER, NEW YORK

PAINTING 1955. (1955). OIL ON CANVAS, 60 × 60" (152.4 × 152.4 CM).
COLLECTION MR. AND MRS. FRANCIS K. LLOYD

ABSTRACT PAINTING, 1956, 80 × 70. (1956). OIL ON CANVAS, 80 × 70″ (203.2 × 177.8 CM).
PRIVATE COLLECTION, SWITZERLAND

94

ABSTRACT PAINTING, 1954–59. (1954–59).
OIL ON CANVAS, 108 × 40″ (274.3 × 101.6 CM).
COLLECTION VIRGINIA DWAN

ABSTRACT PAINTING 1956–60. (1956–60). OIL ON CANVAS, 108 × 40″ (274.3 × 101.6 CM).
THE NELSON-ATKINS MUSEUM OF ART, KANSAS CITY, MISSOURI. ACQUIRED THROUGH THE GENEROSITY OF
PAUL ROSENBERG (BY EXCHANGE), THE RENEE CLEMENTS CROWELL TRUST,
AND THE NELSON GALLERY FOUNDATION, 89–17

PAINTING. (1956–60). OIL ON CANVAS, 108 × 40″ (274.3 × 101.6 CM).
PRIVATE COLLECTION, SWITZERLAND

ABSTRACT PAINTING, 1954–60. (1954–60). OIL ON CANVAS, 108⅛ × 40″ (274.6 × 101.6 CM).
THE BROOKLYN MUSEUM, NEW YORK. GIFT OF THE ARTIST, 67.59

BLACK PAINTING. (1962). OIL ON CANVAS, 60 × 60″ (152.4 × 152.4 CM).
COLLECTION MR. AND MRS. GILBERT H. KINNEY

ABSTRACT PAINTING, NO. 5, 1962. (1962). OIL ON CANVAS, 60 × 60″ (152.4 × 152.4 CM).
TATE GALLERY, LONDON

ABSTRACT PAINTING, NUMBER 33. (1963). OIL ON CANVAS, 60 × 60″ (152.4 × 152.4 CM).
WHITNEY MUSEUM OF AMERICAN ART, NEW YORK. 50TH ANNIVERSARY GIFT OF FRED MUELLER, 80.33

ABSTRACT PAINTING, 1960–1965. (1960–65). OIL ON CANVAS, 60 × 60″ (152.4 × 152.4 CM).
LANNAN FOUNDATION, LOS ANGELES

Abstract Painting. (1963). OIL ON CANVAS, 60 × 60″ (152.4 × 152.4 CM).
THE MUSEUM OF MODERN ART, NEW YORK. GIFT OF MRS. MORTON J. HORNICK

ABSTRACT PAINTING, 1964, 60 × *60.* (1964). OIL ON CANVAS, 60 × 60″ (152.4 × 152.4 CM).
PRIVATE COLLECTION, SWITZERLAND

ABSTRACT PAINTING. (1960). OIL ON CANVAS, 60 × 60″ (152.4 × 152.4 CM).
COLLECTION MICHAEL AND JUDY OVITZ

AD REINHARDT, 1966.

CHRONOLOGY, SELECTED WRITINGS, AND CARTOONS BY AD REINHARDT

CHRONOLOGY

1913 **Born, New York, Christmas Eve, nine months after Armory Show. (Father leaves ''old country'' for America in 1907 after serving in Tsar Nicholas' army. Mother leaves Germany in 1909.)**

1913 *Malevich paints first geometric-abstract painting.*

1914 *Matisse paints ''Porte-Fenêtre, Collioure.''*

1914 *Mondrian begins ''plus-minus'' paintings.*

1915 **Gets crayons for birthday, copies ''funnies,'' Moon Mullins, Krazy Kat and Barney Google.**

1916 *Juan Gris paints ''Dish of Fruit.''*

1916 *Dada in Zurich.*

1917 **Cuts up newspapers. Tears pictures out of books.**

1917 *October Revolution in Russia. Lenin replaces Kerensky.*

1918 *Malevich paints ''White on White.''*

1918 *Peace. World War I ends.*

1919 **Enters Public Grade School No. 88, Fresh Pond Road, Ridgewood, Queens.**

1919 *Léger paints ''The City.''*

1919 *Monet paints ''Water Lilies.''*

1920 **Wins water color flower painting contest.**

1921 *Abstract painters have trouble in Russia.*

1922 *Mexican painters issue anti-''art for art's sake'' manifesto.*

1922 *Joyce completes ''Ulysses.''*

1923 *Marcel Duchamp gives up painting.*

1924 **Copies Old English and German Black-Letter printing.**

1925 *Arp makes ''Mountain, Table, Anchors, Navel.''*

1926 *Picasso paints ''The Studio.''*

1927 **Wins medal for pencil-portraits of Jack Dempsey, Abraham Lincoln, Babe Ruth and Charles Lindbergh.**

1928 **Enters Newtown High School, Elmhurst, Queens.**

1928 **Wins prizes and medals for art and citizenship.**

1929 *Museum of Modern Art opens.*

1929 *Stock Market crashes.*

1929 *Georgia O'Keefe paints ''Black Cross, New Mexico.''*

1930 **Makes drawings of knights, heraldry, shields, stars, battleflags.**

1931 **Enters Columbia College.**

1932 **Paints studies of Michelangelo's Sistine Ceiling figures for literature class of Raymond Weaver who suggests courses with Meyer Schapiro who suggests joining campus radical groups.**

1933 **Falls asleep in all of Irwin Edman's lectures on aesthetics.**

1933 **Thrown off wrestling team for not keeping in training.**

1934 **Accused by Dean Hawkes of stuffing dormitory tenth-floor shower-drains with art materials and flooding ninth floor (not guilty).**

1935 **Elected to Student Board on campaign promise to abolish fraternities.**

1935 **Makes ''cubist-mannered'' cartoon of ''rectilinear'' President Nicholas Murray Butler beating ''curvilinear'' babies with a big club, censored by Jester Editor Herman Wouk, but printed in Spectator by Editor James Wechsler, becomes city-wide ''academic freedom'' issue.**

1935 **Becomes Editor of Jester. Elected to All-American Staff of College Comic Editors.**

1936 *Civil War in Spain.*

1936 **Studies painting with Carl Holty and Francis Criss.**

1936 **Studies painting with Karl Anderson at National Academy.**

1937 **Joins Artists' Union and American Abstract Artists.**

1937 **Hired on Federal Art Project by Burgoyne Diller, becomes ''Artist, Class 1, Grade 4, $87.60 mo., Easel Division.''**

1937 **Marches on all-night picket-lines.**

1938 **Listens to neighbor Stuart Davis' loud ragtime jazz records, looks at his loud colored shirts on clotheslines.**

1938 **Begins series of bright colored paintings.**

1939 **Disagrees with Matta about importance in art of artists rubbing against sweaty people in subway rush-hours.**

1939 **Debates social-protest painters about ''Art of the Museums'' vs. ''Art in the Streets.''**

1940 **Demonstrates in the street against Museum of Modern Art for being against modern art.**

1940	Writes letter against Wyndham Lewis for being against abstract art.	1949	*Irish Republic established.*
1940	Starts to break up geometric paintings of late thirties.	1949	Paints water colors in Virgin Islands waiting for divorce.
1941	Fired from Federal Art Project.	1950	Edits book with Robert Motherwell.
1941	Visits Balcomb Greene's country nudist-colony, runs around naked.	1950	Protests with "Irascibles" against Metropolitan Museum for being against avant-garde art.
1941	Attacked by Mike Gold in Daily Worker.	1950	Makes cartoon called "Abstraction Crowned at the Whitney."
1942	Designs magazines for New York Yankees and Brooklyn Dodgers.	1951	Argues with John Sloan about Jackson Pollock in Taos.
1943	Tries to talk Thomas Merton out of becoming a Trappist.	1951	*Matisse cuts up colored papers.*
1943	Refuses to help Arshile Gorky start a camouflage school.	1952	Debates for several weeks on "The Hess Problem" at Artists' Club.

1940 Writes letter against Wyndham Lewis for being against abstract art.

1940 Starts to break up geometric paintings of late thirties.

1941 Fired from Federal Art Project.

1941 Visits Balcomb Greene's country nudist-colony, runs around naked.

1941 Attacked by Mike Gold in Daily Worker.

1942 Designs magazines for New York Yankees and Brooklyn Dodgers.

1943 Tries to talk Thomas Merton out of becoming a Trappist.

1943 Refuses to help Arshile Gorky start a camouflage school.

1943 Wonders what Adolph Gottlieb and Mark Rothko are up to when they announce, "There is no such thing as good painting about nothing."

1943 Continues making paintings about nothing.

1944 Makes cartoon for Ruth Benedict's pamphlet "Races of Mankind" which Congressman tries to censor for armed-forces distribution because drawing shows Adam with navel. Time magazine reprints Michelangelo's Adam with navel, settling nation-wide "freedom of opinion" issue.

1944 *Liberation of Paris.*

1944 Is first artist to use Collage in daily newspaper (after Max Ernst).

1944 Begins art history studies with Alfred Salmony.

1944 Paints midnights to mornings.

1944 Has first Art Gallery Show at Artists' Gallery.

1945 *Peace. World War II ends.*

1945 Discharged, honorably, from U.S. Navy.

1945 *Civil War in China.*

1946 First show at Betty Parsons Gallery.

1946 Attacks E.E. Cummings for comments on Krazy Kat.

1946 Fired from Newspaper PM.

1947 *India gains independence.*

1947 Begins teaching at Brooklyn College.

1948 Helps found Artists' Club but doesn't help paint walls or sweep floors.

1948 *Israel gains independence.*

1948 Talks at "Subjects of the Artists" School on "Detachment and Involvement" against all involvements.

1949 *Irish Republic established.*

1949 Paints water colors in Virgin Islands waiting for divorce.

1950 Edits book with Robert Motherwell.

1950 Protests with "Irascibles" against Metropolitan Museum for being against avant-garde art.

1950 Makes cartoon called "Abstraction Crowned at the Whitney."

1951 Argues with John Sloan about Jackson Pollock in Taos.

1951 *Matisse cuts up colored papers.*

1952 Debates for several weeks on "The Hess Problem" at Artists' Club.

1952 *Farouk abdicates Egyptian throne.*

1953 Gives up principles of asymmetry and irregularity in painting.

1953 Paints last paintings in bright colors.

1953 Visits Greece.

1954 Daughter born.

1954 *Cambodia, Laos, Vietnam achieve independence.*

1954 *Macdonald Wright returns to Abstract Art.*

1955 Listed in Fortune magazine as one of top twelve investments in Art market.

1956 Borrows money from bank to travel.

1956 *Suez crisis.*

1956 Makes last cartoon, a mandala.

1957 Willem DeKooning says in the Chuckwagon, "The rich are all right."

1957 Buys Pearl Bailey's record, "They're good enough for me."

1957 Forms SPOAF (Society for the Protection of Our Artist Friends) (from themselves), after reading "Nature in Abstraction" statements.

1958 Creates first Non-Happening, shows two thousand color-slides at Artists' Club.

1958 Visits Japan, India, Persia, Egypt.

1959 *Castro Revolution in Cuba.*

1959 *U.S. makes first radar contact with Venus.*

1960 Writes about Buddha images.

1960 *France explodes nuclear bomb.*

1961 Visits Turkey, Syria, Jordan.

1961 *Bay of Pigs fiasco.*

1961	**Protests Guggenheim Museum's "Abstract Expressionist and Imagist" history.**

1961 **Protests Guggenheim Museum's "Abstract Expressionist and Imagist" history.**

1962 **Protests Whitney Museum's "Geometric Abstraction" history.**

1962 **Plan for "Ad Reinhardt Museum" is projected.**

1962 *Algerian independence.*

1962 **Speaks at First Conference on Aesthetic Responsibility.**

1963 **Dissents from Dissent magazine's dissent from "Art-** ists' Committee to Free Siqueiros" from prison.

1963 *Profumo Scandal in England.*

1963 **Six paintings in New York and six paintings in Paris get marked up and have to be roped off from the public.**

1964 **Ten paintings in London get marked up.**

1964 *China explodes atomic bomb.*

1965 *Man walks in space.*

1966 **One hundred twenty paintings at Jewish Museum.**

COMPILED BY AD REINHARDT FOR THE RETROSPECTIVE EXHIBITION CATALOGUE
BY LUCY LIPPARD, *AD REINHARDT: PAINTINGS* (NEW YORK: THE JEWISH MUSEUM, 1966).

ARTISTS' SYMPOSIUM, 1950. CLOCKWISE: SEYMOUR LIPTON, NORMAN LEWIS, JAMES ERNST, PETER GRIPPE, ADOLPH GOTTLIEB, HANS HOFMANN, ALFRED H. BARR, JR., ROBERT MOTHERWELL, RICHARD LIPPOLD, WILLEM DE KOONING, IBRAM LASSAW, JAMES BROOKS, AD REINHARDT, RICHARD POUSETTE-DART

HOW TO LOOK AT MODERN ART IN AMERICA

by Ad Reinhardt

Here's a guide to the galleries—the art world in a nutshell—a tree of contemporary art from pure (abstract) "paintings" (on your left) to pure (illustrative) "pictures" (down on your right). If you know what you like but don't know anything about art, you'll find the artists on the left hardest to understand, and the names on the right easiest and most familiar (famous). You can start in the cornfields, where no demand is made on you and work your way up and around. Be especially careful of those curious schools situated on that overloaded section of the tree, which somehow think of themselves as being both abstract and pictorial (as if they could be both today). The best way to escape from all this is to paint yourself. If you have any friends that we overlooked, here are some extra leaves. Fill in and paste up...

"The time is out of joint"—Hamlet (Shakespeare) ~~~~~~ "Folks are better than angels"—Taylor OOOOO "Art is long, and (space)-time is fleeting"—Longfellow ~~~~~ "Movies are the Best pictures"—Reinhardt

PUBLISHED IN *P.M.*, JUNE 2, 1946.

HOW TO LOOK AT MODERN ART IN AMERICA

by Ad Reinhardt

Here's a guide to the galleries—the art world in a nutshell—a tree of contemporary art from pure (abstract) "paintings" (on your left) to pure (illustrative) "pictures" (down on your right). If you know what you like but don't know anything about art, you'll find the artists on the left hardest to understand, and the names on the right easiest and most familiar (famous). You can start in the cornfields, where no demand is made on you and work your way up and around. Be especially careful of those curious schools situated on that overloaded section of the tree, which somehow think of themselves as being both abstract and pictorial (as if they could be both today). The best way to escape from all this is to paint yourself. If you have any friends that we overlooked, here are some extra leaves. Fill in and paste up...

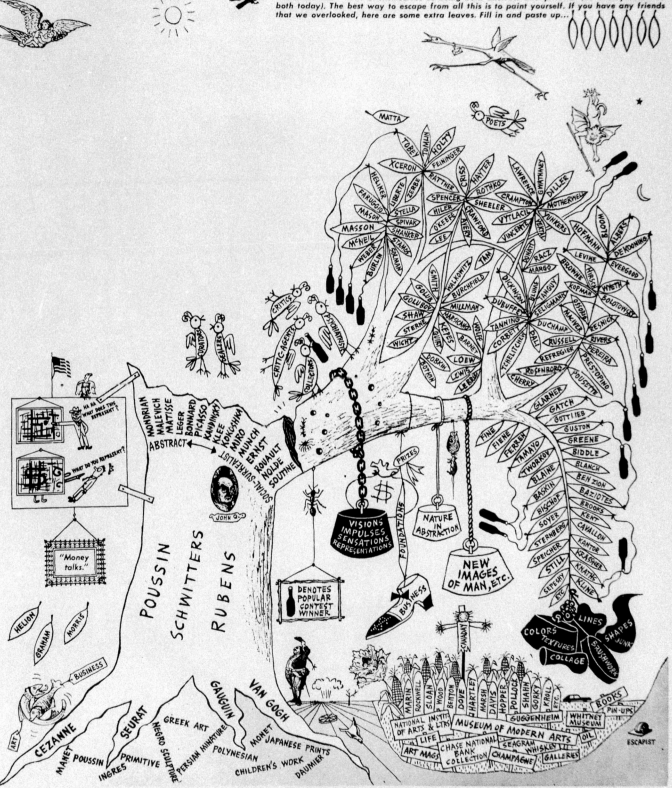

*ARTNEWS apologizes for Mr. Reinhardt for 15 years of misspelling the names Kokoschka, Krasner and O'Keeffe.

111

AD REINHARDT, 1947

ARTIST AS... MAGICIAN, SORCERER, MASTERER, IMAGER
SERVILE, MECHANICAL, CRAFTS, SLAVE LABOR, ANONYMOUS
   GREECE, ROME, MEDIEVAL
12C "SERVANT OF GOD", MYSTIC, ILLUMINATOR, MOSAICIST
14C NO DISTINCTION, ARTIST-ARTISAN   FILIPPO-LIPPI
15C "SERVANT OF GOD IN NATURE", INDIVIDUAL, LEARNED MAN   VAN EYCK
16C SCIENTIST, NATURALIST, "LIBERAL ARTS", RENAISSANCE   DURER
   "DIVINE ARTIST", INNER IDEAL   MICHELANGELO, LEONARDO
17C SERVANT OF THE COURT, "PAINTER TO THE KING"   VELASQUEZ
   NOBLE, CLASSICIST, ROYAL ACADEMY, BEAUX ARTS   POUSSIN
   VELASQUEZ, "THE PERFECT PAINTER", PAINTERS' PAINTER"
      NOT CRAFT OR PROFESSION, RETURNED MONEY TO POPE.
      WORKED VERY LITTLE, STUDIO WORK, EFFORTLESS, CONSCIOUS
      NO SKETCHES, NO ADVENTURES-LIFE, NO INNER STRESS
      PURE VISUAL ENTITIES, SELF-SUFFICIENT, PASSIVE, MUTE
      LEAST SENTIMENTAL, MOST COOLY ARISTOCRATIC, LEAVES US ALONE
      PERSONALLY NOT PRESENT, NO STYLIZATION, NO EXPRESSION
      PURE SEEING, ALL PAINTING INTO PORTRAITURE
      NO IMAGINATION, PROFANE, NO SUBLIME, NO ECSTASY
      ABSENCE INTO PRESENCE, HOVERING BEING, NOT-BEING

18C IDEALIST, "PERFECTIONIST" RATIONALIST, ACADEMICIAN   REYNOLDS
   "PERSONALITY", MYSTIC, ROMANTIC, VIRTUOSO   BLAKE
19C MATERIALIST, NATURALIST, REALIST, "OBSERVER"   DELACROIX
                                                          COURBET
   "IMPRESSIONIST", SPECTATOR, DOCUMENTOR, TRANSFORMER   MANET
   AMATEUR-DILETTANTE, BOURGEOIS-BOHEMIAN   MONET
   DEMOCRAT, BUSINESSMAN, PROFESSIONAL   VERMEER
20C "EXPRESSIONIST", REFLECTOR, PROJECTOR, COMMENTATOR
   ECCENTRIC, PROTESTER, ESCAPIST, EXILE, SATIRIST   REMBRANDT
   CLOWN, PROSTITUTE, ACROBAT, ENTERTAINER   CARAVAGGIO
   "VICTIM", MARTYR, CHRIST, "EXISTENTIALIST"   "NOBLE SAVAGE"
   PRIMITIVE, CHILD, "NEUROTIC", "INNOCENT", "IDIOT", WILD-MAN, FAUVE
   "SYMBOLIST", DREAMER, IMAGER, "SURREALIST", TRICKSTER
   METAPHYSICIAN, MYSTIC, PRIEST, SAINT, MAGICIAN, MONK
   "CELEBRITY", ACTIONIST, VISIONARY   "SUCCESS-FAILURE"
   "MAN", EVERYMAN, INDIVIDUAL, EDUCATOR, TEACHER, SPECIAL-HUMAN
   SCHIZOID, SICK-HEALTHY, PART OF EVERYONE, CRISIS, UNCONSCIOUS
   HERO, CREATOR, GOD, INVENTOR, MASTER, PHILOSOPHER-KING
   GENTLEMAN-SCHOLAR-PRINCE-MONK-HERMIT-"OUTLAW"
                           CONSCIENCE, CONSCIOUSNESS
→ ARTIST-AS-ARTIST
   PURE ARTIST
   ABSTRACT ARTIST

HOW TO LOOK AT ART-TALK

by Ad Reinhardt

Eighth of a series on why a modern painting is not a picture...

"Build your art horse-high, pig-tight and bull-strong" —Hubbard

"How weak is painting to describe a man." —Charles Lamb

"Art is a weapon" —Reinhardt

"... One of the most powerful motives that attract people to science and art is the longing to escape from everyday life." —Einstein

"To wake the soul by tender strokes of art" —Pope

Do artists who draw people like people? Do artists who like people draw people?

NO

Can people be squeezed out of a tube of paint on to a canvas in a frame, huh?

NOPE

Do you like pictures of people in magazines and movies?

YOU BET

Painters paint easel-paintings to exhibit—not to sell, don't they?

YEAH

Has fine-art any relation to prices, profits, private property and social prestige?

WELL ...

57th ST.

KOOTZ GALLERY

PAINTINGS FOR A COUNTRY ESTATE $100 EACH

ACA GALLERY

PAINTINGS FOR A TENEMENT FLAT $1000 EACH

Is a painting a practical means of propaganda today with all our newspapers, movies and radio?

NO

Is a genuine-oil-painted-gilt-framed-picture any great bargain?

NAH

Were not pictures freed from phony "artistic" pretentions so that they could become better pictures?

SURE

Was not painting freed from a "picture-purpose" so that it could become freer and more imaginative?

YEP

Isn't abstract art "just a design," just "composition," just an empty bucket into which one can drop some subject-matter?

NO

Then the purpose and meaning of a painting is in the structure and activity of its lines, shapes and colors, hey?

YEAH

114

DOCUMENTS OF MODERN ART

Reprinted from It Is, *a Magazine of Abstract Art*
Two Quotations from the Old Ecole de Paris and the New
American Academy

"My painting represents the victory of the forces of light and
peace over the powers of darkness and evil."
—*Picasso,* 1958

"My painting represents the victory of the forces of darkness and peace over the powers of light and evil."
—*Reinhardt,* 1957

ARCHIVES OF AMERICAN ART

Censored from It Is, *a Magazine of Abstract Art*
Ten Quotations from the Old New York School

"Voyaging into the night, one knows not where, on an
unknown vessel, an absolute struggle with the elements of
the real."   —*Robert Motherwell,* 1959
"Voyaging into the nought, one knows exactly where, on a
known vessel, an absolute harmony with the elements of
the unreal."   —*Ad Reinhardt,* 1959

"There is no such thing as a good painting about nothing."   —*Adolph Gottlieb* and *Mark Rothko,* 1947
"There is no such thing as a good painting about something."   —*Ad Reinhardt,* 1947

"Art never seems to make me peaceful or pure."
—*Willem de Kooning,* 1951
"Art never seems to make me vulgar or violent."
—*Ad Reinhardt,* 1951

"I looked at Picasso until I could smell his armpits."
—*William Baziotes* and *Rudi Blesh,* 1956
"Study the old masters. Look at nature. Watch out for arm-
pits."   —*Ad Reinhardt,* 1956

"Let no man undervalue the implications of this work, or its
power for life, or for death, if it is misused."
—*Clyfford Still,* 1959
"Let no man undervalue the implications of this work, or its
power for cash, or for bad credit, if it is misused."
—*Ad Reinhardt,* 1959

PUBLISHED IN *PAX*, NO. 13, 1960.

TWELVE RULES FOR A NEW ACADEMY

Evil and error in art are art's own "uses" and "actions." The sins and sufferings of art are always its own improper involvements and mixtures, its own mindless realisms and expressionisms.

The humiliation and trivialization of art in America during the last three decades have been the easy exploitations and eager popularizations of art by the American artists themselves. Ashcan and Armory expressionists mixed their art up with life muckraking and art marketing. Social and surreal expressionists of the thirties used art as an "action on the public," but succeeded mainly in expressing themselves, and abstract expressionists of the forties and fifties, using art initially as a "self-expression," succeeded in acting upon the whole world. The business boom of the twenties orphaned the alienated artist, but the Great Depression of the thirties witnessed the tender engagement of art to government. Ten years after that, the ardent marriage of art and business and war was celebrated with Pepsi-Cola in ceremonial contests called "Artists for Victory" at America's greatest museum of art. By the fifties, armies of art's offsprings were off to school and Sunday school, crusading for art education and religious decoration.

From "Artists for Ashcan and Dust Bowl" to "Artist for America-First and Social Security" to "Artists for Victory" to "Artists for Action in Business, Religion, and Education." The portrait of the artist in America in the twentieth century shapes up into a figure resembling Al Capp's Available Jones, who is always available to anyone, any time, for anything at all, at any price.

(The "ice has been broken," the ivory tower flooded by unschooled professionals, the walls of the academy washed out by schooled primitives, and the sanctum sanctorum blasphemed by fauve folk, Bauhaus bacchuses, and housebroken samurai.)

The conception of art as "fine," "high," "noble," "free," "liberal," and "ideal" has always been academic. The argument of free or fine artists has never been between art and something else, but "between true art and art submitted to some other, quite different, values." "There are not two arts, there is only one." "No man can embrace true art till he has explored the cast out false art." The academy of art, whether the Western or Eastern ideal, has always aimed at "the correction of the artist," not "the enlightenment of the public." The idea of the "academy" of art in the seventeenth century, of "aesthetics" in the eighteenth, of the "independence" of art in the nineteenth, and of the "purity" of art in the twentieth, restate, in those centuries in Europe and America, the same "one point of view." Fine art can only be defined as exclusive, negative, absolute, and timeless. It is not practical, useful, related, applicable, or subservient to anything else. Fine art has its own thought, it own history and tradition, its own reason, its own discipline. It has its own "integrity" and not someone else's "integration" with something else.

Fine art is not "a means of making a living" or "a way of living a life." Art that is a matter of life and death cannot be fine or free art. An artist who dedicates his life to art, burdens his art with his life and his life with his art. "Art is Art, and Life is Life."

The "tradition" of art is art "out of time," art made fine, art emptied and purified of all other-than-art meanings, and a museum of fine art should exclude everything but fine art. The art tradition stands as the antique-present model of what has been achieved and what does not need to be achieved again. Tradition shows the artist what not to do. "Reason" in art shows what art is not. "Higher education for the artist should be 'liberal,' 'free' and the 'learning of greatness.'" "To teach and enlighten is the task of wise and virtuous men." "No great painter was ever self-taught." "Artists must learn and learn to forget their learning." "The way to know is to forget."

"The guardian of the true tradition in art" is the academy of fine art: "to give certain rules to our art and to render it pure." The first rule and absolute standard of fine art, and painting, which is the highest and freest art, is the purity of it. The more uses, relations, and "additions" a painting has, the less pure it is. The more stuff in it, the busier the work of art, the worse it is. "More is less."

The less an artist thinks in non-artistic terms and the less he exploits the easy, common skills, the more of an artist he is. "The less an artist obtrudes himself in his painting, the purer and clearer his aims." The less exposed a painting is to a chance public, the better. "Less is more."

The Six Traditions to be studied are: (1) the pure icon; (2) pure perspective, pure line, and pure brushwork; (3) the pure landscape; (4) the pure portrait; (5) the pure still life; (6) pure form, pure color, and pure monochrome. "Study ten thousand paintings and walk ten thousand miles." "Externally keep yourself away from all relationships, and internally, have no hankerings in your heart." "The pure old men of old slept without dreams and waked without anxiety."

The Six General Canons or the Six Noes to be memorized are: (1) No realism or existentialism. "When the vulgar and commonplace dominate, the spirit subsides." (2) No impressionism. "The artist should once and forever emancipate himself from the bondage of appearance." "The eye is a menace to clear sight." (3) No expressionism or surrealism. "The laying bare of oneself," autobiographically or socially, "is obscene." (4) No fauvism, primitivism, or brute art. "Art begins with the getting rid of nature." (5) No constructivism, sculpture, plasticism, or graphic arts. No collage, paste, paper, sand, or string. "Sculpture is a very mechanical exercise causing much perspiration, which, mingling with grit, turns into mud." (6) No *"trompe-l'oeil,"* interior decoration, or architecture. The ordinary qualities and common sensitivities of these activities lie outside free and intellectual art.

The Twelve Technical Rules (or How to Achieve the Twelve Things to Avoid) to be followed are:

1. No texture. Texture is naturalistic or mechanical and is a vulgar quality, especially pigment texture or impasto. Palette knifing, canvasstabbing, paint scumbling and other action techniques are unintelligent and to be avoided. No accidents or automatism.

2. No brushwork or calligraphy. Handwriting, hand-working and hand-jerking are personal and in poor taste. No signature or trademarking. "Brushwork should be invisible." "One should never let the influence of evil demons gain control of the brush."

3. No sketching or drawing. Everything, where to begin and where to end, should be worked out in the mind beforehand. "In painting the idea should exist in the mind before the brush is taken up." No line or outline. "Madmen see outlines and therefore they draw them." A line is a figure, a "square is a face." No shading or streaking.

4. No forms. "The finest has no shape." No figure or fore- or background. No volume or mass, no cylinder, sphere or cone, or cube or boogie-woogie. No push or pull. "No shape or substance."

5. No design. "Design is everywhere."

6. No colors. "Color blinds." "Colors are an aspect of appearance and so only of the surface." Colors are barbaric, unstable, suggest life, "cannot be completely controlled," and "should be concealed." Colors are a "distracting embellishment." No white. "White is a color and all colors." White is "antiseptic and not artistic, appropriate and pleasing for kitchen fixtures, and hardly the medium for expressing truth and beauty." White on white is "a transition from pigment to light" and "a screen for the projection of light" and "moving" pictures.

7. No light. No bright or direct light in or over the painting. Dim, late afternoon absorbent twilight is best outside. No chiaroscuro, "the malodorant reality of craftsmen, beggars, topers with rags and wrinkles."

8. No space. Space should be empty, should not project, and should not be flat. "The painting should be behind the picture frame." The frame should isolate and protect the painting from its surroundings. Space divisions within the painting should not be seen.

9. No time. "Clock-time or man's time is inconsequential." There is no ancient or modern, no past or future in art. "A work of art is always present." The present is the future of the past, not the past of the future. "Now and long ago are one."

10. No size or scale. Breadth and depth of thought and feeling in art have no relation to physical size. Large sizes are aggressive, positivist, intemperate, venal, and graceless.

11. No movement. "Everything else is on the move. Art should be still."

12. No object, no subject, no matter. No symbols, images, or signs. Neither pleasure nor paint. No mindless working or mindless non-working. No chess-playing.

Supplementary regulations to be followed are: No easel or palette. Low, flat, sturdy benches work well. Brushes should be new, clean, flat, even, one-inch wide, and strong. "If the heart is upright, the brush is firm." No noise. "The brush should pass over the surface lightly and smoothly" and silently. No rubbing or scraping. Paint should be permanent, free of impurities, mixed into and stored in jars. The scent should be "pure spirits of turpentine, unadulterated and freshly distilled." "The glue should be as clear and clean as possible." Canvas is better than silk or paper, and linen is better than cotton. There should be no shine in the finish. Gloss reflects and relates to the changing surroundings. "A picture is finished when all traces of the means used to bring about the end have disappeared."

The fine-art studio should have a "raintight roof" and be twenty-five feet wide and thirty feet long, with extra space for storage and sink. Paintings should be stored away and not continually looked at. The ceiling should be twelve feet high. The studio should be separate from the rest of the school.

The fine artist should have a fine mind, "free of all passion, ill-will and delusion."

The fine artist need not sit cross-legged.

117

PUBLISHED IN *ART NEWS*, MAY 1957.

THE NEXT REVOLUTION IN ART
(Art-as-Art Dogma, Part II)

The next revolution in art will be the same, old, one revolution.

Every revolution in art turns over art from art-as-also-something-else into art-as-only-itself.

The one, eternal, permanent revolution in art is always a negation of the use of art for some purpose other than its own. All progress and change in art is toward the one end of art as art-as-art.

An avant-garde in art advances art-as-art or it isn't an avant-garde.

Art-as-art is as old as art and artists. Artists have always practiced, if not always professed, secretly or openly, art-as-art as artists. Artists-as-artists have always worked the same way and have always made the same things.

Art-as-art is always a battle cry, polemic, picket sign, sit-in, sit-down, civil disobedience, passive resistance, crusade, fiery cross, and non-violent protest.

The artist-as-artist's first enemy is the philistine-artist, the "all-too-human" or subhuman or superhuman artist inside or outside or beside himself, the socially useful and usable artist, the artist-jobber and sales artist, the expressionist-businessman and "action" artist, the artist who "has to eat," who has to "express himself," and who lives off, on, in, for or from his art."

The artist-as-artist's second enemy is the art dealer who deals in art, the private collector who collects art, in other words, the public profiteer who profits from art.

The artist-as-artist's third enemy is the utilitarian, acquisitive, exploiting society in which any tendency to do anything for its own transcendental sake cannot be tolerated.

Art-as-art has always been and always will be a trouble for philosophers, priests, politicians, professors, patriots, provincials, property people, proud possessors, primitives, poets, psychiatrists, petit-bourgeois persons, pensioneers, patrons, plutocrats, paupers, panderers, pecksniffs, and pleasure-seekers, for the reason of art's own Reason that needs no other reason or unreason.

The three most important, principled battles of our time for art against museums took place in New York City at the beginning of each of the last three decades:

In 1940, the battle for modern art was fought on the forty- or fifty-artist picket line of the American Abstract Artists group questioning the "modernity" of the Museum of Modern Art and protesting its "use" of Renaissance art against modern artists. The Museum has shown little Renaissance or medieval or ancient art since.

In 1950, the battle for fine art was fought by a few gallery groupings of artists, numbering around twenty "irascible" artists, petitioning and questioning the wisdom of the Metropolitan Museum of Art's sponsoring of "Pepsi-Cola art" and "I-Hear-America-Singing" ideas of nationalism and regionalism. The Metropolitan Museum has shown little wisdom since.

By 1960, the battle for free or abstract art was being fought by artists, numbering now perhaps only one, privately protesting the Modern Museum's "New American Painting," the Whitney Museum's "Geometric Art in America," and the Guggenheim Museum's "American Expressionist and Imagist" exhibitions, for using the ideas and history of abstract art to support and promote a vulgar, postexpressionist, postsurrealist "pop abstraction." The museums have shown little respect for the main stream of modern art before or since.

For one moment in the early sixties, a group of young artists calling themselves the Artists' Tenant Association struck terror into the heart of the art world by proposing an artists' boycott of New York City's galleries and museums. The artists were fighting for freedom from harassment by the fire department in their lofts merely, but the threat of an artists' strike, even by artists who were not in galleries or museums, showed how the foundations could be shaken.

The most barefaced, half-assed sham battle in the market place in recent years was the "Action Painters' Protest against the Critic of *The New York Times*," with the artists listing themselves shamelessly with their customers, mouthpieces, devotees, and agents. What was good for the actionary artists' busy-art-business was good also for the "embattled" reactionary art critic's busy-book-business, and showed how the foundations could not be shaken.[1]

The next revolution in art will see the disappearance of personal art dealing, private art collecting, and individual artist enterprising, of personalistic, privateering art—"pricing and buying and selling." International art cartels will drive

---

[1] Letter to *New York Times* protesting John Canaday's anti-avant-garde criticism.

out small art business from the top down, and conscience-stricken artists will organize themselves to strike against art-dealers' associations from the bottom up.

The next revolution will wipe out the art-market bird-watchings and callings, and remove the menace of pigeon-droolings, starling-warblings, and "peep"-happenings. The old abstract-expressionist game of "buttonholing and bag-ging the clammy green-bird" with its old bird call of "sweat-ing cubism out" went almost out of fashion even before the heroic Nixon years were over. A late fifties period which was a "sweating the green-bird parrot out" was followed by an early sixties period which heard the howling rosen-bird and his action bats and starlings out. The elimination of the hawkings, buzzardings, nest-featherings and fowlings of the tawney-hess pippett and flank-harrow sparrow, the emily-jinn-hour harpy and cackling coo, the canny-day common crow and larking-allways chicken, the robin gull-water duck and hilly-creamer vampire, and the simp-hunter redden-rut-man gooney species of chutzpah canaries would help to restore the artists' health and sanity and peace of mind, but nature is not so easily deflowered.

The next revolution will sound the farewell of the old favorite songs of "art and life" that the old favorite artist-ducks love to sing along with the old bower-birds and the new, good, rich swallow audiences. What curator has not thrilled to the strains and old refrains of "Art is a style of living, so to speak" (de Kooning, 1951), "Painting is voyaging into the night, one knows not where . . ." (Motherwell, 1959), *"There is no such thing as a painting about nothing"* (Rothko, Gottlieb, 1947), and "Let no man undervalue the implications of this work, or its power for life, or for death, if it is misused" (Still, 1959)? The next revolution will over-throw natural, brute, expressionist, folk, monster, neo-primi-tive, junk, collage, assemblage, combine, mongrel, "merz," "pop," happening, unconscious, spontaneous, accidental, poetic, dramatic, "song-and-dance" art and send it back to the everyday theater and environment, to the entertainment field and junkyard, to the folk places and lower depths where it all came from in the first place.

The next revolution will see a scattering to the winds of all local and foreign New York School "pictures of the pass-ing world" and the permanent acknowledgement of univer-sal "pure land school" paintings everywhere, come heller or high water.

The next revolution will see the fading away of all old, unschooled, "school of hard knocks" artists telling young artists they need not go to school, and the casting to the dogs of all schooled artist company men and the techniques of their trade—brushworking, panhandling, backscratching, palette-knifing, waxing, buncombing, texturing, wheedling, tooling, sponging, carping, blobbing, beefing, staining, straining, scheming, striping, stripping, bowing, scraping, hacking, poaching, subliming, *shpritzing,* soft-soaping, pid-dling, puddling, imaging, visioning, etc. The soft sell on the clean hard edge by the new artists was as much of a sellout as the hard sell on the soft edge was by the dirty old artists.

The next revolution will see the emancipation of the university academy of art from its market-place fantasies and its emergence as "a center of consciousness and con-science," and the formation of a government department of art as the main support of unsupportable art. Art as an art program or art project will be a creeping socialist hot-house flower instead of the present private-enterprise outhouse harlotree.

The next revolution in art will recognize the inalienable right of each art to be free from all other arts, to be free to be itself, and to be free of itself.

Art-as-art is a concentration on art's essential nature. The nature of art has not to do with the nature of perception or with the nature of light or with the nature of space or with the nature of time or with the nature of mankind or with the nature of society or with the nature of the universe or with the nature of creation or with the nature of nature.

Art's nature fixes a boundary that separates it from every-thing else. Anything cannot be art.

Art's "three thousand odd rules" cannot be learned by the "ten thousand creatures." Anybody cannot be an artist.

Art-as-art is the "school of the invariable way" and does not belong to the "ten manners" or to the "hundred schools" or to the "ten thousand things." Art-as-art turns each way into the one way. There are no two ways about it.

Art-as-art is a creation that revolutionizes creation and judges itself by its destructions. Artists-as-artists value themselves for what they have gotten rid of and for what they refuse to do.

Art has never ruled the world.

Art-as-art cannot win the world without losing its soul.

Art's reward is its own virtue.

119

PUBLISHED IN *ART NEWS*, FEBRUARY 1964. ALSO PUBLISHED (UNDER THE TITLE "ART-AS-ART DOGMA, PART II") IN *ART INTERNATIONAL*, MARCH 1964.

A PORTEND OF THE ARTIST AS A YHUNG MANDALA (1955). COLLAGE OF INK AND PAPER. 20 ¼ × 13 ½″ (51.4 × 34.3 CM). COLLECTION OF THE WHITNEY MUSEUM OF AMERICAN ART, NEW YORK. ANONYMOUS GIFT. 76.45. ORIGINALLY PUBLISHED IN *ART NEWS*, MAY 1956.

"ART-AS-ART"

The one thing to say about art is that it is one thing. Art is art-as-art and everything else is everything else. Art-as-art is nothing but art. Art is not what is not art.

The one object of fifty years of abstract art is to present art-as-art and as nothing else, to make it into the one thing it is only, separating and defining it more and more, making it purer and emptier, more absolute and more exclusive—non-objective, non-representational, non-figurative, non-imagist, non-expressionist, non-subjective. The only and one way to say what abstract art or art-as-art is, is to say what it is not.

The one subject of a hundred years of modern art is that awareness of art of itself, of art preoccupied with its own process and means, with its own identity and distinction, art concerned with its own unique statement, art conscious of its own evolution and history and destiny, toward its own freedom, its own dignity, its own essence, its own reason, its own morality and its own conscience. Art needs no justification with "realism" or "naturalism," "regionalism" or "nationalism," "individualism" or "socialism" or "mysticism," or with any other ideas.

The one content of three centuries of European or Asiatic art and the one matter of three millennia of Eastern or Western art, is the same "one significance" that runs through all the timeless art of the world. Without an art-as-art continuity and art-for-art's-sake conviction and unchanging art spirit and abstract point of view, art would be inaccessible and the "one thing" completely secret.

The one idea of art as "fine," "high," "noble," "liberal," "ideal" of the seventeenth century is to separate fine and intellectual art from manual art and craft. The one intention of the word "aesthetics" of the eighteenth century is to isolate the art experience from other things. The one declaration of all the main movements in art of the nineteenth century is of the "independence" of art. The one question, the one principle, the one crisis in art of the twentieth century centers in the uncompromising "purity" of art, and in the consciousness that art comes from art only, not from anything else.

The one meaning in art-as-art, past or present, is art meaning. When an art object is separated from its original time and place and use and is moved into the art museum, it gets emptied and purified of all its meanings except one. A religious object that becomes a work of art in an art museum loses all its religious meanings. No one in his right mind goes to an art museum to worship anything but art, or to learn about anything else.

The one place for art-as-art is the museum of fine art. The reason for the museum of fine art is the preservation of ancient and modern art that cannot be made again and that does not have to be done again. A museum of fine art should exclude everything but fine art, and be separate from museums of ethnology, geology, archaeology, history, decorative arts, industrial arts, military arts, and museums of other things. A museum is a treasure house and tomb, not a counting-house or amusement center. A museum that becomes an art curator's personal monument or an art-collector-sanctifying establishment or an art-history manufacturing plant or an artists' market block is a disgrace. Any disturbance of a true museum's soundlessness, timelessness, airlessness, and lifelessness is a disrespect.

The one purpose of the art academy university is the education and "correction of the artist"-as-artist, not the "enlightenment of the public" or the popularization of art. The art college should be a cloister-ivyhall-ivory-tower-community of artists, an artists' union and congress and club, not a success school or service station or rest home or house of artists' ill-fame. The notion that art or an art museum or art university "enriches life" or "fosters a love of life" or "promotes understanding and love among men" is as mindless as anything in art can be. Anyone who speaks of using art to further any local, municipal, national, or international relations is out of his mind.

The one thing to say about art and life is that art is art and life is life, that art is not life and that life is not art. A "slice-of-life" art is no better or worse than a "slice-of-art" life. Fine art is not a "means of making a living" or a "way of living a life," and an artist who dedicates his life to his art or his art to his life burdens his art with his life and his life with his art. Art that is a matter of life and death is neither fine nor free.

The one assault on fine art is the ceaseless attempt to subserve it as a means to some other end or value. The one fight in art is not between art and non-art, but between true and false art, between pure art and action-assemblage art, between abstract and surrealist-expressionist anti-art, between free art and servile art. Abstract art has its own integrity, not someone else's "integration" with something else. Any combining, mixing, adding, diluting, exploiting, vulgarizing, or popularizing abstract art deprives art of its

121

essence and depraves the artist's artistic consciousness. Art is free, but it is not a free-for-all.

The one struggle in art is the struggle of artists against artists, of artist against artist, of the artist-as-artist within and against the artist-as-man, -animal, or -vegetable. Artists who claim their artwork comes from nature, life, reality, earth or heaven, as "mirrors of the soul" or "reflections of conditions" or "instruments of the universe," who cook up "new images of man"—figures and "nature-in-abstraction"—pictures, are subjectively and objectively rascals or rustics. The art of "figuring" or "picturing" is not a fine art. An artist who is lobbying as a "creature of circumstances" or logrolling as a "victim of fate" is not a fine master artist. No one ever forces an artist to be pure.

The one art that is abstract and pure enough to have the one problem and possibility, in our time and timelessness, of the "one single grand original problem" is pure abstract painting. Abstract painting is not just another school or movement or style but the first truly unmannered and untrammeled and unentangled, styleless, universal painting. No other art or painting is detached or empty or immaterial enough.

The one history of painting progresses from the painting of a variety of ideas with a variety of subjects and objects, to one idea with a variety of subjects and objects, to one subject with a variety of objects, to one object with a variety of subjects, then to one object with one subject, to one object with no subject, and to one subject with no object, then to the idea of no object and no subject and no variety at all. There is nothing less significant in art, nothing more exhausting and immediately exhausted, than "endless variety."

The one evolution of art forms unfolds in one straight logical line of negative actions and reactions, in one predestined, eternally recurrent stylistic cycle, in the same all-over pattern, in all times and places, taking different times in different places, always beginning with an "early" archaic schematization, achieving a climax with a "classic" formulation, and decaying with "late" endless variety of illusionisms and expressionisms. When late stages wash away all lines of demarcation, framework, and fabric, with "anything can be art," "anybody can be an artist," "that's life," "why fight it," "anything goes," and "it makes no difference whether art is abstract or representational," the artists' world is a mannerist and primitivist art trade and suicide-vaudeville, venal, genial, contemptible, trifling.

The one way in art comes from art working and the more an artist works the more there is to do. Artists come from artists, art forms come from art forms, painting comes from painting. The one direction in fine or abstract art today is in the painting of the same one form over and over again. The one intensity and the one perfection come only from long and lonely routine preparation and attention and repetition. The one originality exists only where all artists work in the same tradition and master the same convention. The one freedom is realized only through the strictest art discipline and through the most similar studio ritual. Only a standardized, prescribed, and proscribed form can be imageless, only a stereotyped image can be formless, only a formularized art can be formulaless. A painter who does not know what or how or where to paint is not a fine artist.

The one work for a fine artist, the one painting, is the painting of the one-size canvas—the single scheme, one formal device, one color-monochrome, one linear division in each direction, one symmetry, one texture, one free-hand brushing, one rhythm, one working everything into one dissolution and one indivisibility, each painting into one overall uniformity and non-irregularity. No lines or imaginings, no shapes or composings or representings, no visions or sensations or impulses, no symbols or signs or impastos, no decoratings or colorings or picturings, no pleasures or pains, no accidents or ready-mades, no things, no ideas, no relations, no attributes, no qualities—nothing that is not of the essence. Everything into irreducibility, unreproducibility, imperceptibility. Nothing "usable," "manipulatable," "salable," "dealable," "collectible," "graspable." No art as a commodity or a jobbery. Art is not the spiritual side of business.

The one standard in art is oneness and fineness, rightness and purity, abstractness and evanescence. The one thing to say about art is its breathlessness, lifelessness, deathlessness, contentlessness, formlessness, spacelessness, and timelessness. This is always the end of art.

PUBLISHED IN *ART INTERNATIONAL*, DECEMBER 1962.

39 ART PLANKS:
PROGRAMS FOR "PROGRAM" PAINTING

(Art-as-Art Dogma, Part VII)

1. The re-obliteration of the horizontal band.
2. The re-voidance of the vertical stripe.
3. The re-debarment of line and edge, rough and clean.
4. The re-disappearance of contrast and color.
5. The re-dematerialization of pigment matter.
6. The re-brushing-out of brushwork.
7. The re-blowing-out of hindrances and irregularity.
8. The re-dissolution of the square and cruciform.
9. The re-transfiguration of configuration.
10. The re-denaturalization of neo-naturalism.
11. The re-destruction of neo-constructivism.
12. The re-abstraction of abstraction of abstraction.
13. The re-banishment of the image.
14. The re-Byzantinization of asymmetry.
15. The re-Islamicization of icon and mandala.
16. The re-de-mannerization of neo-mannerism.
17. The re-neo-classicisticization of neo-romanticisticization.
18. The re-de-iconologicalization of iconology.
19. The re-de-meaning of meaning in meaning in art.
20. The re-passification of action and reaction art.
21. The re-domestication of devils "who control the brush" and neo-Dionysiac rascals.
22. The re-de-schematization of spontaneity and variety.
23. The re-stylization of evanescence.
24. The re-de-academicization of chance and accident.
25. The re-revocation of re-stylization and de-schematization.
26. The re-de-expressionisticization and re-"pop-ping" of neo-extract-expressionism.
27. The re-"one-upping" of "op-ping" of "pop-ping."
28. The re-non-objectification of object and subject.
29. The re-de-pictographicization of symbol, signal, and sign.
30. The re-denigration of the production of the reproduction of the reproduction of the production.
31. The re-reformulation of formalism.
32. The re-decontamination of neo-surreal-dada-ism.
33. The re-denuding and re-undoing of the nude and neo-Art-Brut.
34. The re-rejection of the hero-whoreo-artist-man-of-the-world role.
35. The re-categorization of good artists who after long years of hard pushing start pushing bad work.
36. The remonstrance of bad artists who after long years of hard pulling start pulling off good work.
37. The re-establishment of the old classic virtues and a new code of art ethics for artists.
38. The redemption of repentant art and artists.
39. The re-negation of the neo-negation of neo-art-as-art.

PUBLISHED IN *ART VOICES*, SPRING 1963. READ AT THE "DESTRUCTION IN ART SYMPOSIUM," LONDON, 1966.

SHAPE? IMAGINATION? LIGHT?
FORM? OBJECT? COLOR?
WORLD?

SHAPE?

Good shape, bad shape, outlines, edges?
Absolute shape, square?
Horizontal, vertical shapes? Trisections?
Circle as shape, shape as circular, target, sun?
Bull's-eye, God's-eye? Shape of time?
Circular heavens above, endlessness?
Square as shapelessness.

IMAGINATION?

Imagining? Imaging? Imagery? Image?
Imaginary-museum, image of timelessness?
Image of emptiness, empty image?
Imaginationless, fantasyless, surrealistless?
Imagelessness.

LIGHT?

Harsh, soft, reflected, absorbed, transparent light?
Soft lights, sweet music, sweeter unheard music?
Frozen-music architecture? Gothic-Greek light?
Twilight-light, twilight-time, twilight space?
Broken, baroque, dissolved light?
Iridescence, evanescence, transcendence light?
Luminous-numinous? Rome-versus-East light?
Darkness, grayness, greyness, dullness light?
Lightlessness.

FORM?

Spirit, spirit of forms, forms of forms?
Form of forms, formalism, uniform? One form?
Style-cycles, archaic, classic, late forms?
Broken-forms, impressionism, empty forms?
Bad form, good form, right, wrong form?
Form follows function-filthy-lucre?
Form without substance? Without end? Without time?

OBJECT?

Subject, objective, non-objective, non-subjective?
Object of art, object-art, op-art? Antique?
Subjectlessness, matterlessness, thinglessness?
Objectlessness.

COLOR?

Red, white, blue, flying colors?
Green, orange, purple, glossy-black?
Black as color, black as non-color, no-color?
Colorfulness, color interest?
Interest is of no interest in art.

Art-of-color versus art-of-painting?
Color-engineering, color-psychology?
Color-symbolism, symbolic-color, colored-symbols?
Colored crayons, chalks, markers?
Prism, spectrum, rainbow? Color-field?
Race-color, rat-race, dogma-eat-dogma, holy cats?
Topcat, birds of a color feather together?
Horse of a different color?
Hue, tone, tint, tinge, dye, shade, glow, flush, key?
Pigment, wash, distemper, stain, grain, daub?
Pure, primary, primitive, barbaric, emblazon?
Local-color, value, disguise, flesh, blush?
Broken-color, baroque-color, polychromatism?
Full, high, knee-deep, wet, dry, hard, soft, near, far color?
True to one's colors? Guilt-edge, blue-chip?
Color as anti-art.

Monochrome, tone down, wash out, bleach, blanch?
Discolored, pallor, pallid, pale?
Dull, cold, muddy, leaden, wan, dun, sallow?
Dead, dingy, ashen, lack-lustre?
Blackness, darkness, chiaroscuro?
Jet, ink, ebony, coal, pitch, soot, charcoal, ivory, lamp?
Right and wrong, wrong color, makes-no-difference?
Colorlessness.

PUBLISHED IN *PROPHETIC VOICES: IDEAS AND WORDS ON REVOLUTION*,
ED. NED O'GORMAN (NEW YORK: RANDOM HOUSE, 1969).

WORLD?

World of art, art-world, world-art?
Best of all possible worlds?
Primary-world, secondary-world?
Free, non-servile, fine, non-applied world?
Pure, ideal, intellectual, useless, timeless world?
Art-world, ivory-tower, control-tower, art-control?
Wheelers-dealers-world? Collectors-world?
Art-words-world, art-critics, art-critters world?
World of business-before-pleasure and vice-versa?
Living, living-it-up, living-it-down, art-world?
Art whorls, whirls, whoreo-heros, parts, rolls?
Painting is more than the scum of its pots?
Can't you tell your impasto from a holy ground?
Holy smoke.

World-art, all-art, all-of-art, universal-art?
Museum-world, museology, museum-without-walls?
World-of-color-slides, images, pictures, signs, symbols?
Wonders-of-the-world, world-travel, wonder of art?
Wonderful world of Disneyland?
World of imagelessness, voices of silence?
Action-arts speak louder than voids.

The-other-world, this-world, second-hand-world?
Day-in-day-out-day-to-day-routine, ritual-world?
Inner-world, all-in-the-mind, nothing-out-there?
Outside-world, world-outside-window, watch out?
Anti-world, anti-matter, anti-texture?
Other-worldly, anti-worldling, anti-happening?
Out-of-this-world world, the other side of creation?
Worldlylessness.

ART IN ART IS ART-AS-ART

(Art-as-Art Dogma, Part III)

The beginning in art is not the beginning.
Creation in art is not creation.
Nature in art is not nature.
Art in nature is not nature.
The nature of art is not nature.
Art in life is not life.
Life in art is not life.

People in art are not people.
Dogs in art are dogs.
Grass in art is not grass.
A sky in art is a sky.
Things in art are not things.
Words in art are words.
Letters in art are letters.
Writing in art is writing.
Messages in art are not messages.
Explanation in art is not explanation.

Knowledge in art is not knowledge.
Learning in art is not learning.
Ignorance in art is ignorance.
Art-schooling is not schooling.
Unlearning in art is learning.
The unschooled in art are unschooled.

Wisdom in art is not wisdom.
Foolishness in art is foolishness.
Consciousness in art is consciousness.
Unconsciousness in art is unconsciousness.

The picture of art is not a picture.
A work of art is not work.
Working in art is not working.
Work in art is work.
Not working in art is working.
Play in art is not play.
Business in art is business.
Art in business is business.

The substance of art is not substance.
The matter of art is not matter.
The subject of art is not the subject.
The object of art is not the object.
The manner of art is not the manner.
Technique in art is technique.
Qualities in art are qualities.

Order in art is not order.
Chaos in art is chaos.
Symmetry in art is not symmetry.
Asymmetry in art is asymmetry.
A square in art is not a square.
A circle in art is a circle.
A triangle in art is a triangle.
A trisection in art is not a trisection.

A color in art is not a color.
Colorlessness in art is not colorlessness.
Blue in art is blue.
Red in art is red.
Yellow in art is yellow.
Dark gray in art is not dark gray.
Matte black in art is not matte black.
Gloss black in art is gloss black.
White in art is white.

A line in art is not a line.
A wiggly line in art is a wiggly line.
A shape in art is a shape.
A blob in art is a blob.
Form in art is not form.
The formlessness of art is not formlessness.
Imagelessness in art is imagelessness.
Non-imagelessness in art is non-imagelessness.

Limits in art are not limits.
No limits in art are limits.
Discipline in art is discipline.
Sameness in art is not sameness.
Variety in art is not variety.
Monotony in art is not monotony.
Balance in art is not balance.
Freedom in art is freedom.

Drawing in art is drawing.
Graphic art is graphic.
A print in art is a print.
A reproduction in art is a reproduction.

Painting in art is not painting.
Plumbing in art is not plumbing.
Carpentry in art is carpentry.
Texture in art is texture.
Figures in art are figures.
Configurations in art are configurations.
Transfigurizations in art are not transfigurations.

Simplicity in art is not simplicity.
Less in art is not less.
More in art is not more.
Too little in art is not too little.
Too large in art is too large.
Too much in art is too much.
Junk in art is junk.
Informal art is informal.
Brute art is brute.
Tachist art is Tachist.

Action art is action.
Chutzpah in art is chutzpah.
Chance in art is not chance.
Accident in art is not accident.
Spontaneity in art is not spontaneity.
Pushing in art is pushing.
Pulling in art is pulling.
Heroism in art is not heroism.
Hankering in art is hankering.
Hungering in art is hungering.

The perfection of art is not perfection.
The purity of art is not purity.
The idealism of art is not idealism.
The realism of art is not realism.
The corruption of art is corruption.
Compromise in art is compromise.
Food in art is not food.

A collage in art is a collage.
Paste in art is paste.
Paint in art is not paint.
Brushwork in art is brushwork.
Sand, string, plaster in art is sand, string, plaster.
Sculpture in art is sculpture.
Architecture in art is not architecture.

Literature in art is literature.
Poetry in art is poetry.
Music in art is not music.
Poetry in art is not poetry.
Sublimity in art is not sublimity.
Rusticity in art is rusticity.

A sign in art is a sign.
A symbol in art is a symbol.
The symbol of art is not a symbol.
The sign of art is not a sign.
The image of art is not an image.

Vision in art is not vision.
The visible in art is visible.
The invisible in art is invisible.
The visibility of art is visible.
The invisibility of art is visible.

The mystery of art is not a mystery.
The unfathomable in art is not unfathomable.
The unknown in art is not the unknown.
The beyond in art is not beyond.
The immediate in art is not the immediate.
The behind in art is not the behind.
The forefront of art is forefront.

The cosmology of art is not cosmology.
The psychology of art is not psychology.
The philosophy of art is not philosophy.
The history of art is not history.
Art in history is not history.
The meaning of art is not meaning.

The morality of art is not morality.
The religion of art is not religion.
The spirituality of art is not spirituality.
Humanism in art is not humanism.
Dehumanism in art is not dehumanism.
Bumpkin-Dionysianism in art is Bumpkin-Dionysianism.
The iconology of art is not iconology.
The iconoclasm of art is iconoclasm.

Darkness in art is not darkness.
Light in art is not light.
Space in art is space.
Time in art is not time.
Evolution in art is not evolution.
Progress in art is not progress.

The beginning of art is not the beginning.
The finishing of art is not the finishing.
The furnishing of art is furnishing.
The nothingness of art is not nothingness.
Negation in art is not negation.
The absolute in art is absolute.
Art-in-art is art.
The end of art is art-as-art.
The end of art is not the end.

PUBLISHED IN *LUGANO REVIEW*, 1966. ALSO PUBLISHED IN GYORGY KEPES, *SIGN, IMAGE, SYMBOL* (NEW YORK: GEORGE BRAZILLER, 1966).
ANOTHER VERSION OF THIS TEXT APPEARED IN "REINHARDT PAINTS A PICTURE," *ART NEWS*, MARCH 1965.

AD REINHARDT, C. 1950.

EXHIBITION HISTORY

SELECTED ONE-MAN EXHIBITIONS

1943

New York, Teachers College Gallery, Columbia University. "Abstract Gouaches and Collages." December 6–11.

New York, Teachers College Gallery, Columbia University. "Cartoons." March 13–25.

1944

New York, Artists' Gallery. "Abstractions." February 8–26.

1945

New York, Mortimer Brandt Gallery. March.

1946

New York, Art School Gallery, Brooklyn Museum. "Abstract Paintings." March 21–April 18.

New York, Betty Parsons Gallery.

1947

New York, Betty Parsons Gallery. "Abstract Paintings." November 24–December 13.

1948

New York, Betty Parsons Gallery. "Recent Abstract Paintings." October 18–November 6.

1949

New York, Betty Parsons Gallery. "Recent Oil and Casein Paintings." October 31–November 19.

1951

New York, Betty Parsons Gallery. "Recent Oil Paintings." June 4–23.

1952

New York, Betty Parsons Gallery. "Recent Oil Paintings." January 7–26.

1953

New York, Betty Parsons Gallery. "Recent Paintings." November 16–December 5.

1955

New York, Betty Parsons Gallery. "Paintings." January 31–February 19.

1956

New York, Betty Parsons Gallery. "Recent Paintings 1950–1956." November 5–24.

1957

Syracuse, N.Y., Syracuse University Art Gallery. Retrospective exhibition. Fall.

1959

New York, Betty Parsons Gallery. "Paintings." January 5–24.

1960

New York, Betty Parsons Gallery and Section Eleven Gallery. "Twenty Five Years of Abstract Painting." October 17–November 5.

Paris, Galerie Iris Clert. June.

1962

Los Angeles, Dwan Gallery. "Ad Reinhardt." February.

1963

Los Angeles, Dwan Gallery. "Recent Square Paintings, 1960–1963." November–December.

Paris, Galerie Iris Clert. June.

1964

London, Institute of Contemporary Arts. "Ad Reinhardt." Summer.

1965

New York, Graham Gallery. "Paintings, Red, 1950–53." March 2–27.

New York, Betty Parsons Gallery. "Paintings, Black, 1953–65." March 2–27.

New York, Stable Gallery. "Paintings, Blue, 1950–53." March 9–April 3.

1966

New York, The Jewish Museum. "Ad Reinhardt: Paintings." November 23–January 15.

1970

New York, Marlborough Gallery. "Ad Reinhardt: Black Paintings 1951–1967." March 7–April 10.

1972

Düsseldorf, Städtische Kunsthalle. "Ad Reinhardt." September 15–October 15. Traveled to Eindhoven, The Netherlands, Stedelijk van Abbemuseum, December 12–January 1, 1973; Zurich, Kunsthaus, February 11–March 18; Paris, Centre national d'art contemporain, Grand Palais, May 22–July 2; Vienna, Museum des 20. Jahrhunderts.

1974

Milan, Galleria Morone 6. "Ad Reinhardt." June 6–July 1.

New York, Marlborough Gallery. "Ad Reinhardt: A Selection from 1937–1952." March 2–23.

Zurich, Marlborough Galerie. "Ad Reinhardt." November 27–January 31, 1975.

1976

New York, The Pace Gallery. "Ad Reinhardt." October 2–30.

New York, Truman Gallery. "Ad Reinhardt: Art Comics and Satires." October 2–30.

1977

Baden-Baden, West Germany, Staatliche Kunsthalle. "Epitaphe für Ad Reinhardt." November 19–January 8, 1978.

New York, Marlborough Gallery. "Ad Reinhardt: Early Works through Late Black Paintings, 1941–1966." October 15–November 12.

1980

New York, The Solomon R. Guggenheim Museum. "Ad Reinhardt and Color." January 11–March 9.

New York, Marlborough Gallery. "Ad Reinhardt." January 5–26.

New York, Whitney Museum of American Art. "Ad Reinhardt: A Concentration of Works from the Permanent Collection of the Whitney Museum of American Art. A 50th Anniversary Exhibition." December 10–February 8, 1981.

1981

New York, The Pace Gallery. "Ad Reinhardt, 1945–51: Paintings and Watercolors." December 8–January 9, 1982.

1984

Los Angeles, Margo Leavin Gallery. "Ad Reinhardt, Paintings 1937–52." February 23–March 24.

Washington, D.C., The Corcoran Gallery of Art. "Ad Reinhardt: Seventeen Works." September 22–December 16.

1985

Rome, L'Isola s.r.l. "Ad Reinhardt." February. Traveled to Cologne, Karsten Greve Gallery. August.

Stuttgart, Staatsgalerie Stuttgart. "Ad Reinhardt." April 13–June 2.

129

1968

New York, The Museum of Modern Art. "The Art of the Real: USA 1948–1968." July 3–September 8. Traveled to Paris, Grand Palais, November 14–December 23; Zurich, Kunsthaus, January 19–February 23, 1969; London, Tate Gallery, April 24–June 1.

Pasadena, Calif., Pasadena Art Museum. "Serial Imagery." September 17–October 27. Traveled to Seattle, Seattle Art Museum and Santa Barbara, Calif., Santa Barbara Museum of Art.

1969

New York, The Museum of Modern Art. "The New American Painting and Sculpture: The First Generation." June 18–October 5.

Worcester, Mass., Worcester Art Museum. "The Direct Image." October 16–November 30.

1970

Buffalo, N.Y., Albright-Knox Art Gallery. "Color and Field 1890–1970." September 15–November 1. Traveled to Dayton, The Dayton Art Institute, November 20–January 10, 1971; Cleveland, The Cleveland Museum of Art, February 4–March 28.

New York, The Metropolitan Museum of Art. "New York Painting and Sculpture: 1940–1970."

1972

Dallas, Dallas Museum of Fine Arts. "Geometric Abstraction, 1926–1942." October 7–November 19.

Rome, Marlborough Galleria. "American Action Painting." April.

1973

Zurich, Marlborough Galerie AG. "Amerikanische abstrakte Malerei." June–July.

1977

Indianapolis, Indianapolis Museum of Art. "Perceptions of the Spirit in Twentieth-Century American Art." September 20–November 27. Traveled to Berkeley, Calif., University Art Museum, December 20–February 12, 1978; San Antonio, Tex., Marion Koogler McNay Art Institute, March 5–April 16; Columbus, Ohio, Columbus Gallery of Fine Arts, May 10–June 19.

1978

Ithaca, N.Y., Herbert F. Johnson Museum of Art, Cornell University. "Abstract Expressionism: The Formative Years." March 30–May 14. Traveled to Tokyo, The Seibu Museum of Art, June 17–July 12; New York, Whitney Museum of American Art, October 5–December 3.

1981

New York, Whitney Museum of American Art. "Decade of Transition: 1940–50." April 30–July 12.

1984

New York, Whitney Museum of American Art. "Abstract Painting and Sculpture in America 1927–1944." June 27–September 9.

1989

Buffalo, N.Y., Albright-Knox Art Gallery. "Abstraction, Geometry, Painting: Selected Geometric Abstract Painting in America Since 1945." September 17–August 30. Traveled to Miami, Center for the Fine Arts, December 15–February 25, 1990; Milwaukee, Milwaukee Art Museum, April 1–June 1; New Haven, Conn., Yale University Art Gallery, July–September 30.

SELECTED BIBLIOGRAPHY

The books, catalogues, and articles that follow are organized chronologically. Multiple entries in any given year are ordered alphabetically.

BOOKS AND CATALOGUES INCLUDING THE ARTIST

Janis, Sidney, and Grace McCann Morley. *Abstract and Surrealist Art in the United States*. San Francisco: San Francisco Museum of Art, 1944. Exhibition catalogue.

The Intrasubjectives. New York: Kootz Gallery, 1949. Exhibition catalogue.

Ritchie, Andrew Carnduff. *Abstract Painting and Sculpture in America*. New York: The Museum of Modern Art, 1951. Exhibition catalogue.

Degand, Léon. *Regards sur la peinture américaine*. Paris: Galerie de France, 1952. Exhibition catalogue.

Arnason, H. H. *The Classic Tradition in Contemporary Art*. Minneapolis: Walker Art Center, 1953. Exhibition catalogue.

Morley, Grace McCann. *American Art: Four Exhibitions*. Brussels: Brussels Universal and International Exhibition, 1958. Exhibition cataloguo.

New York and Paris: Painting in the Fifties. Houston: Museum of Fine Arts, 1959. Exhibition catalogue.

Arnason, H. H. *60 American Painters*. Minneapolis: Walker Art Center, 1960. Exhibition catalogue.

Ad Reinhardt: Twenty-Five Years of Abstract Painting. New York: Betty Parsons Gallery, 1960. Exhibition catalogue.

Arnason, H. H. *American Abstract Expressionists and Imagists*. New York: The Solomon R. Guggenheim Museum, 1961. Exhibition catalogue.

Art Since 1950. Seattle: Seattle World's Fair, 1962. Exhibition catalogue.

Gordon, John. *Geometric Abstraction in America*. New York: Whitney Museum of American Art, 1962. Exhibition catalogue.

Miller, Dorothy. *Americans 1963*. New York: The Museum of Modern Art, 1963. Exhibition catalogue.

Painting and Sculpture of a Decade: 1954-

64. London: Tate Gallery (with the Calouste Gulbenkian Foundation, Lisbon), 1964. Exhibition catalogue.

Tuchman, Maurice. *New York School: The First Generation, Paintings of the 1940s and 1950s*. Los Angeles: Los Angeles County Museum of Art, 1965. Exhibition catalogue.

Seitz, William C. *The Responsive Eye*. New York: The Museum of Modern Art, 1965. Exhibition catalogue.

Lippard, Lucy. *Ad Reinhardt: Paintings*. New York: The Jewish Museum, 1966. Exhibition catalogue.

10. New York: Dwan Gallery, 1966. Exhibition catalogue.

Lippard, Lucy, Irving Sandler, and G. R. Swenson. *Two Decades of American Painting*. New York: The International Council of The Museum of Modern Art, and Melbourne, Australia: National Gallery of Victoria, 1967. Exhibition catalogue.

Coplans, John. *Serial Imagery*. Pasadena, Calif.: Pasadena Art Museum, 1968. Exhibition catalogue.

Goossen, Eugene. *The Art of the Real: USA 1948-1968*. New York: The Museum of Modern Art, 1968. Exhibition cataloguo.

Rose, Barbara. *American Art Since 1900*. New York and Washington, D.C.: Praeger Publishers, 1968.

Geldzahler, Henry. *New York Painting and Sculpture: 1940-1970*. New York: E. P. Dutton and Co., in association with The Metropolitan Museum of Art, 1969. Exhibition catalogue.

Lucie-Smith, Edward. *Late Modern: The Visual Arts Since 1945*. New York: Praeger Publishers, 1969.

Arnason, H. H., and Barbara Rose. *Ad Reinhardt: Black Paintings, 1951–1967*. New York: Marlborough Gallery, 1970. Exhibition catalogue.

Sandler, Irving. *The Triumph of American Painting: A History of Abstract Expressionism*. New York: Praeger Publishers, 1970.

Ashton, Dore. *The New York School: A Cultural Reckoning*. New York: Penguin, 1972.

Ad Reinhardt. Düsseldorf: Städtische Kunsthalle, 1972. Exhibition catalogue.

Ad Reinhardt. Eindhoven, The Netherlands: Stedelijk van Abbemuseum, 1972. Exhibition catalogue.

Seuphor, Michael, and John Elderfield. *Geometric Abstraction, 1926-1942*. Dallas: Dallas Museum of Fine Arts, 1972. Exhibition catalogue.

Battcock, Gregory, ed. *The New Art: A Critical Anthology*. New York: E. P. Dutton, 1973.

Ad Reinhardt. Paris: Centre national d'art contemporain, 1973. Exhibition catalogue.

McConathy, Dale. *Ad Reinhardt: A Selection from 1937–1952*. New York: Marlborough Gallery, 1974. Exhibition catalogue.

Hess, Thomas B. *The Art Comics and Satires of Ad Reinhardt*. Düsseldorf: Kunsthalle, and Rome: Marlborough, 1975.

Rose, Barbara, ed. *Art-as-Art: The Selected Writings of Ad Reinhardt*. New York: The Viking Press, 1975.

Schjeldahl, Peter. *Ad Reinhardt: Art Comics and Satires*. New York: Truman Gallery, 1976. Exhibition catalogue.

Dillenberger, Jane, and John Dillenberger. *Perceptions of the Spirit in Twentieth-Century American Art*. Indianapolis: Indianapolis Museum of Art, 1977. Exhibition catalogue.

Hobbs, Robert Carleton, and Gail Levin. *Abstract Expressionism: The Formative Years*. Ithaca, N.Y.: The Herbert F. Johnson Museum of Art, Cornell University, 1978. Exhibition catalogue.

Rowell, Margit. *Ad Reinhardt and Color*. New York: The Solomon R. Guggenheim Museum, 1980. Exhibition catalogue.

Sims, Patterson. *Ad Reinhardt: A Concentration of Works from the Permanent Collection*. New York: Whitney Museum of American Art, 1980. Exhibition catalogue.

Lippard, Lucy. *Ad Reinhardt*. New York: Harry N. Abrams, 1981.

Livingston, Jane. *Ad Reinhardt: Seventeen Works*. Washington, D.C.: The Corcoran Gallery of Art, 1984. Exhibition catalogue.

Inboden, Gudrun, and Thomas Kellein. *Ad Reinhardt*. Stuttgart: Staatsgalerie Stuttgart, 1985. Exhibition catalogue.

Battcock, Gregory, ed. *Minimal Art: A Criti-*

cal Anthology. New York: E. P. Dutton, 1986.

Clark, David J. The Influence of Oriental Thought on Postwar American Painting and Sculpture. New York and London: Garland Publishing, 1988.

Auping, Michael. Abstraction, Geometry, Painting: Selected Geometric Abstract Painting in America Since 1945. Buffalo, N.Y.: Albright-Knox Art Gallery and New York: Harry N. Abrams, 1989.

Buchloh, Benjamin. L'Art conceptuel: une perspective. Paris: Musée d'art moderne de la Ville de Paris, 1990.

Colpitt, Frances. Minimal Art: The Critical Perspective. Ann Arbor, Mich.: UMI Research Press, 1990.

Guilbaut, Serge, ed. Reconstructing Modernism: Art in New York, Paris, and Montreal 1945–1964. Cambridge, Mass., and London: The MIT Press, 1990.

ARTICLES ABOUT THE ARTIST

Hess, Thomas B. "Reinhardt: The Position and Perils of Purity." Art News 52 (December 1953): 26–27, 59.

de Kooning, Elaine. "Pure Paints a Picture." Art News 56 (Summer 1957): 57, 86–87.

Tillim, S. "What Happened to Geometry? An Inquiry into Geometrical Painting in America." Arts Magazine 33 (June 1959):38–44.

Ashton, Dore. "Art." Arts & Architecture 77 (December 1960): 4–5.

James, Martin. "Today's Artists: Reinhardt." Portfolio and Art News Annual, no. 3 (1960): 48–63, 140–46.

Colt, Priscilla. "Notes on Ad Reinhardt." Art International 8 (October 20, 1964): 32–34.

Sylvester, David. "Blackish." The New Statesman, June 12, 1964, 924.

"The Black Monk." Newsweek, March 15, 1965, 90.

Lippard, Lucy. "New York Letter." Art International 9 (May 1965): 52–53.

Rose, Barbara. "ABC Art." Art in America 53 (October–November 1965): 57–69.

Wollheim, R. "Minimal Art." Arts Magazine 39 (January 1965): 26–32.

Coates, Robert. "Rejections." The New Yorker, December 10, 1966, 172–76.

Kramer, Hilton. "Ad Reinhardt's Black Humor." New York Times, November 27, 1966, D17.

McShine, Kynaston. "More than Black." Arts Magazine 41 (December 1966–January 1967): 49–50.

Michelson, Annette. "Ad Reinhardt or the Artist as Artist." Harper's Bazaar, November 1966, 176, 223.

Rose, Barbara. "Reinhardt." Vogue, November 1, 1966, 183.

Rosenstein, Harris. "Black Pastures." Art News 65 (November 1966): 33–35.

Sandler, Irving. "Reinhardt: The Purist Backlash." Artforum 5 (December 1966): 40–47.

Ashton, Dore. "Notes on Ad Reinhardt's Exhibition." Arts & Architecture 83 (January 1967): 4–5.

Bourdon, David. "Master of the Minimal." Life, February 3, 1967, 45–52.

Denny, R. "Ad Reinhardt: An Appreciation;" and Phyllis Kallick, "Interview with Ad Reinhardt." Studio 174 (December 1967): 264–73.

Hess, Thomas B. "Ad (Adolph Dietrich Friedrich) Reinhardt." Art News 66 (October 1967): 23.

Lippard, Lucy. "Silent Art." Art in America 55 (January 1967): 58–63.

Lippard, Lucy. "Ad Reinhardt: 1913–1967." Art International 11 (October 1967): 19.

O'Doherty, Brian. "Anti-Matter." Art and Artists, January 1967, 42–44.

Smithson, Robert. "A Museum of Language in the Vicinity of Art." Art International 12 (March 1968): 21–27.

Fuller, M. "Ad Reinhardt Monologue." Artforum 9 (October 1970): 36–41.

Müller, Gregoire. "After the Ultimate." Arts Magazine 44, no. 5 (March 1970): 28–31.

Kozloff, Max. "Andy Warhol and Ad Reinhardt: The Great Accepter and the Great Demurrer." Studio International 181 (March 1971): 113–17.

"The Prize: An Exchange of Letters Between Ajay and Reinhardt." Art in America 59 (November–December 1971): 106–109.

Alloway, Lawrence. "Artists as Writers, Part Two: The Realm of Language." Artforum 12 (April 1974): 30–35.

Hess, Thomas B. "The Art Comics of Ad Reinhardt." Artforum 12 (April 1974): 47–51.

Howe, S. "The End of Art." Archives of American Art Journal 14 (1974): 2–7.

Lippard, Lucy. "Ad Reinhardt: One Art." Art in America 62 (September–October 1974): 65–75.

Lippard, Lucy. "Ad Reinhardt: One Work." Art in America 62 (November–December 1974): 95–101.

Martin, Richard. "Red in Art is Red." Arts Magazine 48 (April 1974): 40–41.

McConathy, Dale. "Keeping Time: Some Notes on Reinhardt, Smithson and Simonds." artscanada 32 (June 1975): 52–57.

Kramer, Hilton. "Satirizing the Art World." New York Times, October 17, 1976, D27.

Paskus, Benjamin G. "Ad Reinhardt: Art as Art . . . ." Art Journal (Winter 1976–1977): 172–76.

Rosenberg, Harold. "The Art World: Purifying Art." The New Yorker, February 23, 1976, 94–98.

Flagg, Nancy. "The Beats in the Jungle." Lugano Review, September–October 1977, 56–59.

Lippard, Lucy. "Ad Reinhardt: Black Painting." Art and Australia, January–April 1977, 266–68.

Masheck, Joseph. "Cruciformality." Artforum 15 (Summer 1977): 56–63.

Flagg, Nancy. "Reinhardt Revisiting." Art International 22 (February 1978): 54–57.

Friedman, B. H. " 'The Irascibles': A Split Second in Art History." Arts Magazine 53 (September 1978): 54–57.

Beck, James H. "Ad Reinhardt in Retrospect." Arts Magazine 54 (June 1980): 148–50.

Brach, Paul. "Ad Reinhardt: Ultimate Chroma." Art in America 68 (March 1980): 96–99.

Larson, Kay. "Classicist in an Expressionist Era." *Art News* 75 (April 1980): 60–61.

McConathy, Dale. "Ad Reinhardt: 'He Loved to Confuse and Confound.'" *Art News* 79 (April 1980): 56–59.

Ratcliff, Carter. "Mostly Monochrome." *Art in America* 69 (April 1981): 111–131.

Firestone, Evan R. "James Joyce and the First Generation New York School." *Arts Magazine* 56 (June 1982): 116–21.

McEvilley, Thomas. "Heads It's Form, Tails It's Not Content." *Artforum* 12 (November 1982): 50–61.

Parmesani, Lorena. "From Life to Death from Death to Life." *Flash Art*, no. 117 (April–May 1984): 56–61.

Richardson, Elizabeth. "Considering Reinhardt." *Artweek* 15, no. 11 (March 17, 1984): 3.

Shikes, R. E., and S. Heller. "The Art of Satire: Painters as Caricaturists and Cartoonists." *Print Review* 19 (1984): 114–18.

Marcadé, Bernard. "This Never-Ending End . . ." *Flash Art*, no. 124 (October–November 1985): 36–39.

Madoff, S. H. "Vestiges and Ruins. Ethics and Geometric Art in the Twentieth Century." *Arts Magazine* 61 (December 1986): 36.

Lebenszteijn, Jean-Claude. "Framing Classical Space." *Art Journal* 47 (Spring 1988): 37–41.

Ratcliff, Carter. "Dandyism and Abstraction in a Universe Defined by Newton." *Artforum* 27 (December 1988): 87–88.

Morris, Robert. "Three Folds in the Fabric and Four Autobiographical Asides as Allegories: or Interruptions." *Art in America* 77 (November 1989): 144–45

ACKNOWLEDGMENTS

It is with great pleasure that The Museum of Contemporary Art and The Museum of Modern Art present this exhibition and publication of the work of the influential abstract painter Ad Reinhardt. Since the 1966–67 exhibition of his work at The Jewish Museum in New York, galleries and museums around the world have presented various aspects of Reinhardt's art. None, however, has attempted as comprehensive a showing as this one, which encompasses every phase of Reinhardt's oeuvre.

"Ad Reinhardt" presents the work of an artist who was one of the most-traveled and most art-historically informed American painters of his generation, and whose production included not only paintings, gouaches, and collages, but satirical cartoons and a large body of writings on art. Often associated with the New York School, Reinhardt was also an important influence on the Minimalist and Conceptual artists of the 1960s and 1970s.

The retrospective presents approximately ninety-five works dating from 1938 to 1966, nearly all of which are documented in this publication. Organized chronologically, it traces the artist's development from the Cubist-derived, geometric abstractions of the 1930s, through his exploration of all-over abstraction in the 1940s, to the series of monochromatic paintings characterized by symmetrical blocks of blue or red done between 1952 and 1954. This last group led to the vertical "black" paintings of the mid- to late 1950s and, finally, to the "black" five-foot squares that were his preoccupation until his death in 1967.

This exhibition and publication mark the first formal collaboration between The Museum of Modern Art and The Museum of Contemporary Art. "Ad Reinhardt" is co-organized by William Rubin, Director Emeritus of the Department of Painting and Sculpture at The Museum of Modern Art, and Richard Koshalek, Director of The Museum of Contemporary Art. With this exhibition, both curators realize a long-standing desire to present the work of Reinhardt, a project very much overdue.

The intensive curatorial effort required to organize this retrospective would not have been possible without the contributions of Lynn Zelevansky, Curatorial Assistant in the Department of Painting and Sculpture at The Museum of Modern Art, and Alma Ruiz, Assistant Curator for this exhibition at The Museum of Contemporary Art. Both have been integrally involved in all phases of the exhibition from research to realization. Their creative insights into Reinhardt's work and their indefatigable efforts have contributed significantly to the character and shape of this ambitious project.

The organization of this exhibition required the effort and cooperation of numerous individuals. First and foremost, we would like to express our profound gratitude to the artist's widow, Rita Reinhardt-Bedford, and to his daughter, Anna Reinhardt. Their unflagging dedication to this endeavor and gracious accessibility and assistance throughout its planning were crucial to its success. Rita Reinhardt-Bedford's remarkable memory and unusually evenhanded insights into Reinhardt's history made her an invaluable resource. She was also extremely helpful in such practical matters as locating works in private collections and facilitating their loan.

Arnold Glimcher of The Pace Gallery, New York, has been exceedingly generous, not only in lending many works to the exhibition, but also in permitting access to those portions of the gallery's records that were germane to this project. Thanks are due especially to Renato Danese, Director, whose advice and curatorial insight were invaluable, and Melissa M. Brooks, Archivist, who was continually called upon for assistance and who always provided it cheerfully. The staff of Marlborough Gallery in London and Pierre Levai of Marlborough Gallery in New York graciously and efficiently responded to numerous telephone calls and requests for photographs and transparencies, and we are most grateful for their help.

Special appreciation goes to Lucy Lippard, whose extensive knowledge of the artist proved of inestimable value. Robert Irwin, Ellsworth Kelly, Joseph Kosuth, and Stephen Prina also very kindly shared revealing insights into Reinhardt's work from their personal perspectives.

The quality of an exhibition is only as high as the generosity of its lenders permits it to be. This is felt particularly keenly in this case, where the delicacy of Reinhardt's works might have threatened the realization of this endeavor. We are deeply grateful for the support of Mr. and Mrs. Gilbert H. Kinney, who selflessly allowed us to borrow numerous works from what is the most formidable Reinhardt collection in private hands. Robert and Jane Meyerhoff lent extremely generously from their superb collection, and we are in their debt. We also very much appreciate the kindness of Mr. and Mrs. Charles H. Carpenter, Jr., in lending from their fine collection of Reinhardts. The Museum of Modern Art is especially gratified to be able to include in this exhibition a major painting from Mr. and Mrs. Gifford Phillips that is a promised gift to the Museum. In addition, we would like to express our deepest appreciation to all of the private lenders and public institutions whose names appear on page 141. For

LENDERS TO THE EXHIBITION

The Brooklyn Museum, New York

Albright-Knox Art Gallery, Buffalo, New York

The Art Institute of Chicago

The Nelson-Atkins Museum of Art, Kansas City, Missouri

Tate Gallery, London

Lannan Foundation, Los Angeles

The Montclair Art Museum, New Jersey

Yale University Art Gallery, New Haven, Connecticut

The Metropolitan Museum of Art, New York

The Museum of Modern Art, New York

Whitney Museum of American Art, New York

The Carnegie Museum of Art, Pittsburgh

Museum of Art, Rhode Island School of Design, Providence, Rhode Island

The Virginia Museum of Fine Arts, Richmond

The Corcoran Gallery of Art, Washington, D.C.

National Gallery of Art, Washington, D.C.

Anne and Joel Ehrenkranz

Milly and Arne Glimcher

William Greenspon

Mr. and Mrs. Gilbert H. Kinney

Mr. and Mrs. Francis K. Lloyd

Linda and Harry Macklowe

Robert and Jane Meyerhoff

Joan and Fred Nicholas

The Oliver-Hoffmann Collection

Michael and Judy Ovitz

Jesse Philips

Mr. and Mrs. Gifford Phillips

Kathy and Keith Sachs

Denise and Andrew Saul

Mr. and Mrs. John Martin Shea

Marcia S. Weisman

Anonymous lenders

Richard Brown Baker Collection

Irving Blum

Mr. and Mrs. Charles H. Carpenter, Jr.

Mr. and Mrs. Charles M. Diker

Virginia Dwan

Edward Tyler Nahem Fine Art, New York

The Pace Gallery, New York

Manny Silverman Gallery, Los Angeles

143

PHOTOGRAPH CREDITS AND PERMISSIONS